OCR GCSE Religious Studies A
World Religion(s)

Christianity

Katie Clemmey · Pamela Draycott · Janet Dyson
Gordon Kay · Liz Pope · Cavan Wood

Series Editor: Janet Dyson
Series Consultant: Jon Mayled

D1638862

www.heinemann.co.uk
✓ Free online support
✓ Useful weblinks
✓ 24 hour online ordering

01865 888080

Official Publisher Partnership

OCR AND HEINEMANN ARE WORKING TOGETHER TO PROVIDE BETTER SUPPORT FOR YOU

Heinemann is an imprint of Pearson Education Limited, a company incorporated in England and Wales, having its registered office at Edinburgh Gate, Harlow, Essex, CM20 2JE. Registered company number: 872828

www.heinemann.co.uk

Heinemann is a registered trademark of Pearson Education Limited Text © Pearson Education Limited 2009

First published 2009

13 12 11 10 09
10 9 8 7 6 5 4 3 2 1

British Library Cataloguing in Publication Data
A catalogue record for this book is available from the British Library

ISBN 978-0-435-50130-3

Edited by Bruce Nicholson
Reviewed by Reverend Paul Hedworth
Proofread by Margaret Christie
Designed by Pearson Education Limited
Project managed and typeset by Wearset Ltd,
Boldon, Tyne and Wear
Original illustrations © Pearson Education Limited 2009
Illustrated by Wearset Ltd, Boldon, Tyne and Wear
Picture research by Q2AMedia
Cover photo/illustration © Elvele Images/Alamy
Printed by Scotprint, UK

Acknowledgements
The author and publisher would like to thank the following individuals and organisations for permission to reproduce photographs:
Page 2 Photodisc/Geostock. Page 6 Mary Evans Picture Library. Page 10 The Gallery Collection/Corbis. Page 12 akg-images. Page 13 Adeleine Openshaw/Shutterstock. Page 14 Wellford Tiller/Shutterstock. Page 16 Titian/The Bridgeman Art Library/ Getty. Page 18 English School, (20th century)/Private Collection/Barbara Singer/The Bridgeman Art Library. Page 26 Peter Dejong/Associated Press. Page 30 Topham/PressNet/ TopFoto. Page 31 Imagebroker/Alamy. Page 38 Cartier/ Jupiterimages. Page 42(a) JTB Photo/Photolibrary. Page 42(b) JTB Photo/Photolibrary. Page 42(c) Mikhail Levit/Shutterstock. Page 42(d) Steve Vidler/Photolibrary. Page 44R Apis/Sygma/ Corbis. Page 44L Associated Press. Page 49 Homer Sykes/ Corbis. Page 50 Gary Cook/Alamy. Page 54L Lefteris Pitarakis/ Associated Press. Page 54R Pearson Education Ltd/Tudor Photography. Page 56 Kathy Collins/Corbis. Page 60 Mary Evans Picture Library. Page 62 Rob Geiffith/Associated Press. Page 65B Helene Rogers/Art Directors & Trip Photo Library. Page 65T Libby Welch/Alamy. Page 66 Theodore Liasi/ Photographersdirect. Page 69 Chigo Roli/Photolibrary. Page 75 Philippe Hays/Alamy. Page 76 Pearson Education Ltd/Tudor Photography. Page 80(a) Sorrie/IstockPhoto. Page 80(b) Helene Rogers/Art Directors & Trip Photo Library. Page 80(c) Kevin Britland/Alamy. Page 82 Tom Joslyn/Photolibrary. Page 83T Philip Lange/Shutterstock. Page 83M John Hemmings/ Shutterstock. Page 83B Cloki/Shutterstock. Page 86 Ghirlandaio, Ridolfo (Bigordi), Il (1483–1561)/National Gallery, London, UK/ The Bridgeman Art Library. Page 87 ZTS/Shutterstock. Page 88 Wojtek Buss/Photolibrary. Page 90 Network Photographer/ Alamy. Page 91 Alfred Eisenstaedt/Stringer/Time & Life Pictures/Getty Images. Page 92 Robert Mulder/Godong/Corbis. Page 94 Wayne Taylor/Associated Press. Page 96 Bettmann/ CORBIS. Page 103 Kenneth Sponsler/Shutterstock. Page 104 Sergei Karpukhin/Reuters. Page 108 Helene Rogers/Art Directors & Trip Photo Library. Page 110 Helene Rogers/Art Directors & Trip Photo Library. Page 112 Jupiterimages. Page 114 Geoff A. Howard/Alamy. Page 116 Tate, London 2009. Page 117 Gerhard Peter/Associated Press. Page 120 Geoff A. Howard/ Alamy. Page 122 Tim Graham Photo Library/Getty Images. Page 127T Cafod. Page 127B Tearfund. Page 127M Libby Welch/ Alamy. Page 128 The Image Works/TopFoto. Page 132 John Baker/Photographersdirect. Page 133 Darrel Giesbrecht/ PhotographersDirect. Page 138 Bjorn Svensson/Photolibrary. Page 140 akg-images. Page 141 MarioPonta/Alamy. Page 142 The Image Works/TopFoto. Page 144 Mark Boulton/Alamy. Page 145 Lebrecht Music & Arts Photo Library/Photolibrary. Page 150 Jupiterimages.

The authors and publisher would like to thank the following for permission to use copyright material:
All scripture quotations taken from The Holy Bible,
New International Version Anglicised
Copyright © 1979, 1984 by International Bible Society.
Used by permission of Hodder & Stoughton Publishers,
a division of Hachette (UK) Ltd.
All rights reserved.
"NIV" is a registered trademark of International Bible Society.
UK trademark number 1448790.

Every effort has been made to contact copyright holders of material reproduced in this book. Any omissions will be rectified in subsequent printings if notice is given to the publishers.

Contents

Introduction

A note for teachers

This Student Book has been written especially to support the OCR Religious Studies Specification A, Units B571: *Christianity 1* (Core beliefs, Special days and pilgrimage, Major divisions and interpretations) and B572: *Christianity 2* (Places and forms of worship, Religion in the faith community and the family, Sacred writings). It is part of an overall series covering the OCR Specification A and comprising:

- a series of Student Books covering Christianity, Christianity from a Roman Catholic Perspective, Islam, Judaism and Perspectives on Christian Ethics – further details on pages viii and ix.
- a series of Teacher Guides: one covering Christianity, Islam and Judaism, and another three covering Buddhism, Hinduism and Sikhism – further details on pages viii and ix.

Who are we?

The people who have planned and contributed to these books include teachers, advisers, inspectors, teacher trainers and GCSE examiners, all of whom have specialist knowledge of Religious Studies. For all of us the subject has a real fascination and we believe that good Religious Studies can make a major contribution to developing the skills, insights and understanding people need in today's world. In the initial development of this series, Pamela Draycott lent us her expertise, which we gratefully acknowledge.

Why is Religious Studies an important subject?

We believe that Religious Studies is an important subject because every area of life is touched by issues to do with religion and belief. Following a Religious Studies GCSE course will enable students to study and explore what people believe about God, authority, worship, beliefs, values and truth. Students will have opportunities to engage with questions about why people believe in God and how beliefs can influence many aspects of their lives.

Students will also explore why members of a particular religion may believe different things. In lessons students will be expected to think, talk, discuss, question and challenge, reflect on and assess a wide range of questions. As young people growing up in a diverse society studying religion will help them to understand and relate to people whose beliefs, values and viewpoints differ from their own, and help them to deal with issues arising, not only in school, but in the community and workplace.

The study of religion will also help students to make connections with a whole range of other important areas, such as music, literature, art, politics, economics and social issues.

The specification for OCR A Christianity

The specification outlines the aims and purposes of GCSE and the content to be covered is divided into six different Topics. The book's structure follows these Topic divisions precisely:

Topic 1: Core beliefs

Topic 2: Special days and pilgrimage

Topic 3: Major divisions and interpretations

Topic 4: Places and forms of worship

Topic 5: Religion in the faith community and the family

Topic 6: Sacred writings

The Topics focus on developing skills such as analysis, empathy and evaluation, which will enable students to gain knowledge and understanding of the specified content.

In following this specification students will have the opportunity to study Christianity in depth and will learn about the diversity and the way in which people who believe in the religion follow its teachings in their everyday lives.

This book covers everything students will need to know for the examination and shows them how to use their knowledge and understanding to answer the questions they will be asked.

Changes to the specification

The specification has changed dramatically according to the developing nature of education and the need to meet the demands of the world for students. The new specification will be taught from September 2009 onwards. The main changes that teachers and students should be aware of include the following:

- The Assessment Objectives (AOs) have changed, with a 50% focus now given to AO1 (Describe, explain and analyse, using knowledge and understanding) and a 50% focus to AO2 (Use evidence and reasoned argument to express and evaluate personal responses, informed insights and differing viewpoints). Previously, the balance was 75% to 25% respectively. There is more information on this on pages x and xi.

- There is an increased focus on learning *from* religion rather than simply learning *about* religion, and explicit reference to religious beliefs is now required in answers marked by Levels of Response.

- Levels of Response grids have been changed to a new range of 0 to 6 marks for AO1 questions and 0–12 marks for AO2 questions. Complete grids can be found on pages x and xi.

- Quality of Written Communication (QWC) is now only assessed on parts (d) and (e) of each question.

- Beyond the six Christianity Topics covered by this book, there is now a greater choice of Topics within the specification including a new Christian Scriptures paper on the Gospels of Mark and Luke, a paper on Muslim texts and a paper on Jewish texts.

- There is also more freedom to study different combinations of religions and Topics.

Why did we want to write these resources?

We feel strongly that there is a need for good classroom resources that take advantage of the changed Assessment Objectives which:

- make the subject lively, interactive and relevant to today's world

- encourage students to talk to each other and work together

- challenge students and encourage them to think in depth in order to reach a high level of critical thinking

- train students to organise their thoughts in writing in a persuasive and structured way, and so prepare them for examination.

The book has many features which contribute towards these goals. **Grade Studio** provides stimulating and realistic exercises to train students in what examiners are looking for and how to meet those expectations. **Exam Café** provides an exciting environment in which students can plan and carry out their revision.

Of course learning is about more than just exams. Throughout the book you will find **Research Notes**, which encourage students to explore beyond the book and beyond the curriculum. All of these features are explained in more detail on the next two pages.

What is in this book?

This Student Book has the following sections:

- **Introduction**, which you are reading now
- Six **Topics** covered in the specification
- **Exam Café** – an invaluable resource for students studying their GCSE in Religious Studies
- **Glossary** – a reference tool for key terms and words used throughout the book.

Each of the above is covered in more detail in the text below.

The six Topics

Each Topic in this book contains:

- a Topic scene-setter (**The Big Picture**)
- a look at the key questions raised by the Topic, and the key words and issues associated with those questions (**Develop your knowledge**)
- two-page spreads covering the **main Topic content**
- two pages of different level questions to check understanding of the Topic material (**Remember and Reflect**)
- exam-style questions with level indicators, examiner's comments and model answers (**Grade Studio**).

These features, which are explained more fully in the following pages, have been carefully planned and designed to draw together the OCR specification in an exciting but manageable way.

The Big Picture

This provides an overview of the Topic. It explains to students **what** they will be studying (the content), **how** they will study it (the approaches, activities and tasks) and

why they are studying it (the rationale). It also includes a **Get started** activity, often linked to a picture or visual stimulus, which presents a task designed to engage students in the issues of the Topic and give them some idea of the content to be studied.

Develop your knowledge

This lists the **key information**, **key questions** and **key words** of the Topic. At a glance, it allows students to grasp the basic elements of knowledge they will gain in the study of the Topic. It is also a useful reference point for reflection and checking information as it is studied.

Main Topic content

The main content of each Topic is covered in a number of two-page spreads. Each spread equates to roughly one lesson of work – although teachers will need to judge for themselves if some of these need more time.

Each spread begins with the **learning outcomes**, highlighted in a box at the top of the page, so that students are aware of the focus and aims of the lesson. The text then attempts to answer, through a balanced viewpoint, one or two of the key questions raised in

Develop your knowledge. The text carefully covers the views of both religious believers and non-believers. It is also punctuated with activities that range from simple tasks that can take place in the classroom to more complex tasks that can be tackled away from school.

A range of margin features adds extra depth and support to the main text both for students and the teacher.

- **For debate** invites students to examine two sides of a controversial issue.
- **Must think about!** directs students towards a key idea that they should consider.
- **Sacred text** provides an extract from the sacred texts of the religion to help students understand religious ideas and teachings.
- **Research notes** provide stimulating ideas for further research beyond the material covered in the book and in the OCR specification.

Activities

Every Topic has a range of interesting activities which will help students to achieve the learning outcomes. Every two-page spread has a short starter activity to grab students' attention and to get them thinking (see **Get Started** activity on page vi). This is followed by a development section where the main content is introduced, and a plenary activity, which may ask students to reflect on what they have learnt, or may start them thinking about the next steps.

All activities are labelled **AO1** or **AO2** so you can tell at a glance which skills will be developed.

Remember and Reflect

This provides an opportunity for students to reflect on what they have learned and identify possible weaknesses or gaps in their knowledge. It also helps them to recognise key ideas in the specification content. Once they have tested their knowledge with the first set of questions, a cross-reference takes them back to the relevant part of the text so they can check their answers. A second set of questions helps them to develop the AO2 skills necessary for the examination.

What is Grade Studio?

Everyone has different learning needs and this section of the book gives clear focus on how, with guidance from the teacher, students can develop the skills that will help them to achieve higher levels in their exam responses.

Grade Studio appears as boxes within each Topic, as well as a two-page spread at the end of every Topic. It includes tips from the examiner, guidance on the steps to completing a well structured answer, and sample answers with examiner comments.

What is the Exam Café?

This is the revision section of the book. Here students will find useful revision tools and tips on how to get started on their revision and exam preparation. Students will also find assessment advice, including examples of different types of questions and samples of frequently asked questions. A useful **revision check list** allows students to review each Topic's content and explains where to find material in the book that relates to the exam questions.

Exam Café also has:

- sample student answers with examiner's comments
- help on understanding exam language, so students can achieve higher grades
- examiner tips, including common mistakes to be avoided.

Heinemann's OCR Religious Studies A Series

Below is a snapshot of the complete OCR Religious Studies A series. Further detail can be found at www.heinemann.co.uk/gcse.

OCR A Teacher Guide – Christianity, Islam and Judaism

ISBN 978-0-435-50136-5

This Teacher Guide covers Christianity, Islam and Judaism. It corresponds throughout to the Student Books and contains lesson plans, worksheets and Grade Studios to provide a complete teaching course for the chosen religion(s). The Christianity section of the Teacher Guide covers each Topic in the specification with six sample lesson plans and worksheets. The other religions have three sample lesson plans and worksheets. Everything is cross referenced to the student books to help you make the most out of these resources.

The Teacher Guide comes with a Resource Browser CD-ROM, which contains all the lesson plans along with a fully customisable version of all the worksheets.

Perspectives on Christian Ethics Student Book

ISBN 978-0-435-50270-6

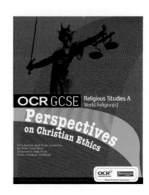

This book provides complete coverage of both units of Christian Ethics (B589 and B603). It provides information, activities, and Grade Studio examples for all aspects of the course, as well as an 8-page Exam Café for revision. Teachers will find support for almost all aspects of this course in the OCR B Teacher Guide: Philosophy and Applied Ethics (ISBN 978-0-435-50152-5)

Roman Catholic Student Book

ISBN 978-0-435-50132-7

This book provides complete coverage of both units of Christianity (Roman Catholic) (B573 and B574). It provides information, activities, and Grade Studio examples for all aspects of the course, as well as an 8-page Exam Café for revision.

Islam Student Book

ISBN 978-0-435-50134-1

This book provides complete coverage of both units of Islam (B577 and B578). It provides information, activities, and Grade Studio examples for all aspects of the course, as well as an 8-page Exam Café for revision. Comprehensive support for the Teacher is provided through the corresponding OCR A Teacher Guide (see above).

Judaism Student Book

ISBN 978-0-435-50133-4

This book provides complete coverage of both units of Judaism (B579 and B580). It provides information, activities, and Grade Studio examples for all aspects of the course, as well as an 8-page Exam Café for revision. Comprehensive support for the Teacher is provided through the corresponding OCR A Teacher Guide (see above).

OCR A Teacher Guide – Buddhism

ISBN 978-0-435-50129-7

This Teacher Guide covers Buddhism. It contains lesson plans, worksheets and Grade Studios to provide a complete teaching course for Buddhism. It covers Units B569 and B570 in the OCR A specification.

OCR A Teacher Guide – Hinduism

ISBN 978-0-435-50128-0

This Teacher Guide covers Hinduism. It contains lesson plans, worksheets and Grade Studios to provide a complete teaching course for Hinduism. It covers Units B575 and B576 in the OCR A specification.

OCR A Teacher Guide – Sikhism

ISBN 978-0-435-50127-3

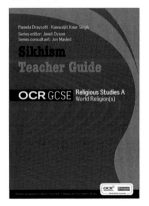

This Teacher Guide covers Sikhism. It contains lesson plans, worksheets and Grade Studios to provide a complete teaching course for Sikhism. It covers Units B581 and B582 in the OCR A specification.

Assessment Objectives and Levels of Response

Assessment Objectives, AO1 and AO2

In the new specification, the questions in the examination are designed to test students against two Assessment Objectives: AO1 and AO2. In the specification 50% of the marks will be awarded for AO1 questions and 50% will be awarded for AO2 questions.

AO1 Questions require candidates to 'describe, explain and analyse, using knowledge and understanding'.

AO2 Questions require candidates to 'use evidence and reasoned argument to express and evaluate personal responses, informed insights, and differing viewpoints'.

Each question in the examination is composed of 5 parts, a–e. In more detail:

- Parts **a–c** are worth one, two and three marks respectively and test a candidate's knowledge (AO1 skills).
- Part **d** is worth six marks and tests a candidate's understanding (AO1 skills).
- Part **e** is worth twelve marks and tests a candidate's AO2 skills.

LEVELS OF RESPONSE FOR MARKING AO1 PART (D) QUESTIONS

LEVEL 1
(1–2 marks)

A **weak** attempt to answer the question.

Candidates will demonstrate little understanding of the question.

- A small amount of relevant information may be included.
- Answers may be in the form of a list with little or no description/explanation/analysis.
- There will be little or no use of specialist terms.
- Answers may be ambiguous or disorganised.
- Errors of grammar, punctuation and spelling may be intrusive.

LEVEL 2
(3–4 marks)

A **satisfactory** answer to the question.

Candidates will demonstrate some understanding of the question.

- Information will be relevant but may lack specific detail.
- There will be some description/explanation/analysis although this may not be fully developed.
- The information will be presented for the most part in a structured format.
- Some use of specialist terms, although these may not always be used appropriately.
- There may be errors in spelling, grammar and punctuation.

LEVEL 3
(5–6 marks)

A **good** answer to the question.

Candidates will demonstrate a clear understanding of the question.

- A fairly complete and full description/explanation/analysis.
- A comprehensive account of the range and depth of relevant material.
- The information will be presented in a structured format.
- There will be significant, appropriate and correct use of specialist terms.
- There will be few, if any, errors in spelling, grammar and punctuation.

LEVELS OF RESPONSE FOR MARKING AO2 PART (E) QUESTIONS

LEVEL 0

(0 marks)

No evidence submitted or response does not address the question.

LEVEL 1

(1–3 marks)

A **weak** attempt to answer the question.

Candidates will demonstrate little understanding of the question.

- Answers may be simplistic with little or no relevant information.
- Viewpoints may not be supported or appropriate.
- Answers may be ambiguous or disorganised.
- There will be little or no use of specialist terms.
- Errors of grammar, punctuation and spelling may be intrusive.

LEVEL 2

(4–6 marks)

A **limited** answer to the question.

Candidates will demonstrate some understanding of the question.

- Some information will be relevant, although may lack specific detail.
- Only one view might be offered and developed.
- Viewpoints might be stated and supported with limited argument/discussion.
- The information will show some organisation.
- Reference to the religion studied may be vague.
- Some use of specialist terms, although these may not always be used appropriately.
- There may be errors in spelling, grammar and punctuation.

LEVEL 3

(7–9 marks)

A **competent** answer to the question.

Candidates will demonstrate a sound understanding of the question.

- Selection of relevant material with appropriate development.
- Evidence of appropriate personal response.
- Justified arguments/different points of view supported by some discussion.
- The information will be presented in a structured format.
- Some appropriate reference to the religion studied.
- Specialist terms will be used appropriately and for the most part correctly.
- There may be occasional errors in spelling, grammar and punctuation.

LEVEL 4

(10–12 marks)

A **good** answer to the question.

Candidates will demonstrate a clear understanding of the question.

- Answers will reflect the significance of the issue(s) raised.
- Clear evidence of an appropriate personal response, fully supported.
- A range of points of view supported by justified arguments/discussion.
- The information will be presented in a clear and organised way.
- Clear reference to the religion studied.
- Specialist terms will be used appropriately and correctly.
- Few, if any, errors in spelling, grammar and punctuation.

Topic 1: Core beliefs

The Big Picture

In this Topic you will be addressing Christian beliefs about:

- the Creeds, especially the Apostles' Creed
- the Trinity, Father, Son and Holy Spirit
- sin, judgement, forgiveness, salvation and eternal life
- the Ten Commandments (Exodus 20:1–17) and the Christian ideal as expressed in Jesus' teaching in the Sermon on the Mount (Matthew 5–7) and the two great commandments (Mark 12:28–34).

You will also think about the ways in which these beliefs affect the life and outlook of Christians in today's world.

What?

You will:

- develop your knowledge and understanding of key Christian beliefs
- find out what these beliefs mean to Christians and think about how they might affect how Christians live
- make links between these beliefs and what you think or believe.

How?

By:

- recalling and selecting information about the key Christian beliefs and explaining their importance to Christians today
- thinking about the relevance of Christian beliefs in the 21st century
- evaluating your own views about these Christian beliefs.

Why?

Because:

- these Christian beliefs underpin, and are reflected in, other aspects of Christian practices (such as in worship and through special ceremonies like funerals)
- understanding Christian beliefs can help you understand why Christians think and act in the way they do
- understanding these beliefs helps you to compare and contrast what others believe, including thinking about your own ideas and beliefs.

Statue of Christ in Rio de Janeiro, Brazil.

🕐 **GET STARTED**

1 Which of these three statements is the odd one out and why?
   • Paris is the capital city of France
   • $229 \times 45.5 = 10,419.5$
   • Manchester United is the best football team in the world.
2 What is the difference between fact, opinion and belief?
3 What is the difference between belief and faith?

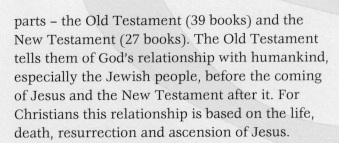

Core beliefs

- Christians are followers of Jesus of Nazareth, also referred to as 'the Christ' ('Christos', a Greek word). 'Christ' means 'the Anointed One'. In the Jewish Scriptures, Messiah referred to a leader whose coming was expected to set up the rule of God on Earth. Christians believe that Jesus is that Messiah.

- It is estimated that there are around 2.1 billion Christians, about a third of the world population. There are over 38,000 different Christian denominations. Different denominations organise their church structures and worship in different ways and interpret differently some elements of Christian doctrine: for example, the Roman Catholic Church teaches that bread and wine become the body and blood of Jesus in the sacrament of the Mass, while generally the Methodist Church teaches that the Lord's Supper is a special remembrance of Jesus where the bread and wine are used symbolically.

- Jesus was a Palestinian Jew who lived about 2000 years ago in the Middle East in the region now known as Israel. Many believe Jesus to have been a holy man, prophet and miracle worker, who taught the possibility of a personal relationship with God through faith.

- A summary of what Christians believe can be found in the Apostles' Creed. A legend says that the Twelve Apostles each wrote one line of the Creed.

- Another important early Christian creed is the Nicene Creed drawn up in 325 CE. The Creed acts as a reminder of the core beliefs that have been passed down from the earliest Christians.

- Christians are monotheists. They believe that there is one God who is revealed in the Trinity.

- The Christian Bible is 66 books written over a 1500-year period. The Bible for Christians is the 'revealed word of God'. The Bible is in two parts – the Old Testament (39 books) and the New Testament (27 books). The Old Testament tells them of God's relationship with humankind, especially the Jewish people, before the coming of Jesus and the New Testament after it. For Christians this relationship is based on the life, death, resurrection and ascension of Jesus.

- A very early statement of commitment was 'Jesus Christ is Lord'. This remains a powerful statement of belief for Christians today.

- From very early times Christians have used the cross as a symbol of their beliefs. It is important because they believe Jesus suffered and died on it. It is a symbol of love, forgiveness and triumph over sin and evil.

- Another early symbol is the fish. Some of the first disciples were fishermen and when Jesus called them he told them they would be 'fishers of men' (Mark 1:16–20). In Greek the word 'fish' is 'ichthus'. This is an acronym. Each letter is the first letter of a word which makes up the statement of faith: Jesus Christ God's Son Saviour.

KNOWLEDGE AND UNDERSTANDING

What do Christians believe about God?

Do Christians really believe in one God or in three Gods?

How can Jesus be both God and human?

ANALYSIS AND EVALUATION

What do I find interesting, or puzzling, about what Christians believe?

What do I believe about God and why do I believe it?

absolution The pronouncement by a priest of the forgiveness of sins.

Ascension The event, 40 days after the Resurrection, when Jesus 'ascended into heaven' (see Luke 24 and Acts 1).

Christ 'The Anointed One'.

Christian A believer in and follower of Jesus.

church The word has three meanings: (i) the building where Christians worship, (ii) the congregation who worship in that building and who go out into the world to serve Jesus, and (iii) the fellowship of all believers.

confession Contrition; penance; (i) one of seven sacraments observed by some Churches whose priests confidentially hear a person's confession; (ii) an admission, by a Christian, of wrong-doing; (iii) a particular official statement (or profession) of faith.

creed Summary statement of religious beliefs, often recited in worship, especially the Apostles' and Nicene Creeds.

eternal life After death the soul will go to heaven and be eternally in the presence of God.

Father One person of the threefold nature of God.

forgiveness The teaching of forgiveness forms part of the most important and widely used Christian prayer – the prayer Jesus taught his disciples, commonly known as the Lord's Prayer.

Heaven The place, or state, in which souls will be united with God after death.

Hell The place, or state, in which souls will be separated from God after death.

Holy Spirit One person of the threefold nature of God.

immanent God is close to and involved with every part of creation.

incarnate The doctrine that God took human form in Jesus.

Jesus of Nazareth The central figure of Christian history and devotion. The second person of the Trinity.

Messiah Used in the Jewish tradition to refer to the expected leader sent by God, who will bring salvation to God's people.

Pentecost Annual festival held to remember the coming of the Holy Spirit. It falls seven weeks after Easter.

repent The first and necessary step towards forgiveness – being truly sorry for the things done or not done and being determined to try to make amends and not to repeat the mistakes (sins).

resurrection The rising from the dead of Jesus Christ on the third day after the crucifixion.

salvation Being saved from sin through belief in Jesus – the healing of a broken relationship between people and God through Jesus.

Son One of the threefold nature of God.

transcendent God is beyond the physical/natural world, outside human understanding.

Trinity Three persons in one God; doctrine of the threefold nature of God – Father, Son and Holy Spirit.

Virgin Birth The doctrine of the miraculous conception of Jesus Christ by the Virgin Mary through the power of the Holy Spirit and without the agency of a human father.

FOR INTEREST Did you know that Jesus ('Isa in the Qur'an) is recognised as a Prophet within Islam?

Muslims believe that 'Isa, like all the Prophets, should be treated with respect. Muslims do not believe that he is divine or that he died on the cross. Muslim belief is that Jesus was raised to heaven by Allah and that he will return at a time close to the Day of Judgement to restore justice and to defeat the Anti-Christ.

The Apostles' Creed

'The Last Supper' by Leonardo da Vinci showing Jesus and the twelve Apostles.

The Apostles' Creed

The Apostles' Creed is a summary of the core beliefs of Christians. Today's version is based on one that was available in the 4th century CE. Legend says that each of the Twelve Apostles wrote one line of the Creed.

It outlines key beliefs about:

- the **Trinity** – 'one God in three persons' – **Father**, **Son** and **Holy Spirit** (See Topic 1.2)
- the importance of the birth, life, death, **resurrection** and **ascension** of **Jesus** and the belief that he will come again
- the importance of the **Church** and the bond between all Christians, living and dead
- belief in eternal life.

In many Christian churches the Apostles' Creed is said regularly as part of worship. It acts as one of the focal points of shared belief.

ACTIVITIES

What do you know about what Christians believe or do? As a class, discuss what is a belief and what is a practice.

Make a class list of 5 to 8 Christian beliefs that you already know something about.

ACTIVITIES

How does the class list of Christian beliefs you drew up compare with the core beliefs of Christianity as laid out in the Apostles' Creed?

Who were the Apostles after which the creed is named?

They were twelve close followers (disciples) of Jesus. They are known as the 'Apostles'. The word 'Apostle' means 'sent out one' or 'messenger'. One of them, Judas Iscariot, betrayed Jesus to the authorities which led to Jesus' arrest and crucifixion. Judas then committed suicide and he was replaced by Matthias. These twelve were very influential in the growth of the early Christian Church.

The Apostles' Creed remains important to Christians today as a 'touchstone of orthodoxy'. What do you think this phrase means?

ACTIVITIES

- What does the Apostles' Creed say about what Christians believe about God and Jesus?
- What do you think the phrases 'holy Catholic Church' and 'the communion of saints' might mean?
- Why is a statement of belief written over 1600 years ago still important to Christians today?
- What do you find interesting or puzzling about what the Apostles' Creed says about what Christians believe?

The Apostles' Creed

I believe in one God, the Father almighty, creator of heaven and earth.

I believe in Jesus Christ, his only Son, our Lord,
who was conceived by the Holy Spirit,
born of the Virgin Mary.
Suffered under Pontius Pilate,
was crucified, died and was buried;
he descended to the dead.
On the third day he rose again,
he ascended into heaven,
he is seated at the right hand of the Father,
and he will come to judge the living and the dead.

I believe in the Holy Spirit,
the holy Catholic Church,
the communion of saints,
the forgiveness of sins,
the resurrection of the body,
and the life everlasting.

Amen.

GradeStudio

AO1

QUESTION

Explain why the Apostles' Creed is important to some Christians. **[6 marks]**

This is an AO1 question, meaning it is trying to test your knowledge and understanding. Examiners will use three levels to measure how successfully you demonstrate these skills. Let's look at what you need to do to achieve a higher level.

The key to this question is the word 'important'. It is often used in exam questions and can have several meanings. Something can be important for practical reasons, because it affects how someone feels, because it affects the way people think or behave, or because it links with other ideas or actions. Better answers will explore different aspects of how something is important. Responses could be built from a simple statement of practical importance such as:

Level 1
The Apostles' Creed is important because it is recited as part of regular worship in church.

Level 2
Go on to explain why it is important in worship, by saying it includes statements of Christian belief and is used to enable all Christians to state their faith openly.

Level 3
To achieve this level, explain that the Apostles' Creed is important, because it is linked with the close followers of Jesus (Apostles) and because it lays down the core beliefs of Christians. It is important as a yardstick against which to measure other statements of belief and from which to develop doctrines. It is also important as a way of drawing Christians together and strengthening the family of the church by stating their beliefs openly in church.

The Trinity

Belief in the Trinity

The Apostles' **Creed** expresses Christian beliefs about the Trinity: that there is one God who is known in three 'persons' – **Father**, **Son** and **Holy Spirit**. Summarised below are the three aspects of the one God. Christians explain their experience of God as:

- Father, the creator and sustainer of heaven and earth – almighty (powerful) – a 'loving parent'.
- Son, God **incarnate** – fully God and fully human. Jesus was born of a human mother and lived a human life (but was sinless). Jesus showed God's love through his teaching and actions, died and rose to life again. Jesus ascended to heaven and at the end of time he will come as judge.
- Holy Spirit, the Power of God at work in the world today.

Belief in the Trinity is a core belief that makes Christianity different from other faiths. Belief in the Trinity does not mean that Christians believe in three Gods. Christians are **monotheists** – they believe in one God.

Different symbolic ways of explaining this belief in the Trinity have been used. Tertullian, a Roman writer in the 2nd century CE, described it as 'the sun sending out rays of sunshine'.

A legend says that when St Patrick was on his mission to evangelise the Irish he used the shamrock as a visual aid to describe the Trinity. Just as the leaf has three parts but is a single leaf – so God is one and yet God is three.

How do Christians describe God?

We have seen that Christians understand God as a Trinity and have explored how this belief is expressed in credal statements. Here we look in more detail at how Christians understand and describe what God is like and how their belief in the Trinity affects their lives.

Although the Trinity can be simplified in symbols such as a trefoil or clover leaf, it is a complex idea which was developed, after much discussion, by Christians during the 4th century CE. The doctrine of the Trinity has been described as one of the most baffling areas of Christian theology. How can Christians think of God as three persons?

To understand the significance of the Trinity you need to remember three key Christian beliefs:

- God created the world.
- God redeemed the world from sin through Jesus.
- God is always present in the world guiding believers through the Holy Spirit.

The next two pages will help you to:

- explain the **Trinity** and what Christians believe about God
- explore some of the attributes of God and how Christians express their beliefs about God
- explore your own beliefs about God.

ACTIVITIES

Look at this image of a shamrock. How might you try to depict Christian belief about the Trinity through a picture?

On his mission to Ireland, St Patrick used the shamrock as a visual aid to describe the Trinity.

These key beliefs are expressed in the concepts of God as creator/Father, Son and Holy Spirit.

- For Christians, God is the creator of all there is. He is the source and sustainer of everything and has an intimate relationship with his creation.
- Calling God 'Father' is a way of showing this belief that God made everything. It is also a way of showing the belief that God loves people as a good father loves his children. Some Christians describe God as 'mother' to show that God has female as well as male qualities.
- Christians believe that **Jesus of Nazareth** was the Son of God. God himself came into the world as a human being in the form of Jesus. This is called the **incarnation**.
- After the death of Jesus, God sent the Holy Spirit into the lives of Christians.

How do Christians express their beliefs about God?

Many Christians recognise that words cannot adequately express what they believe about God. Words often used to describe the characteristics of God include love, goodness, justice, holiness, eternity, beauty, power and glory.

Expressing beliefs through worship

Christians express, share and affirm their beliefs about God through worship. Hymns are often used as a way of helping believers both to praise God and to understand the meaning of teachings about God such as the Trinity. The Grace, said at the end of prayers in most churches, ends with reference to the Trinity: 'In the name of God, the Father, the Son and the Holy Spirit, Amen.'

Expressing beliefs through living

The Christian beliefs that God has created everything, that he involved himself in human history and experience through the life of Jesus **Christ**, and that he is present in the world today through the Holy Spirit, influence strongly how Christians live their lives. Christians believe they have responsibility to live in ways that show care and respect for God's creation and for their fellow humans.

FOR DEBATE

Do you agree with the statement that the concept of the Trinity is baffling? Can you explain it in a way that is easy to understand?

ACTIVITIES

How people perceive their god/gods determines the way they worship and the way they live. People can make anything into a god which they worship in a non-religious sense, money or sport, for example, something they are committed to which takes over their life and becomes their 'religion'. Make a list of non-religious things which could take on the status of a god in some people's lives. How might someone behave if this was the case? Share your examples as a class or group.

God the Father

God giving life to Adam.

Is God like a 'loving parent'? Is God 'the creator'?

'I believe in one God, the Father almighty, creator of heaven and earth.'

The opening sentence of the Apostles' Creed attempts to describe the indescribable – God. It does not attempt to answer the question *Does God exist?* It starts from the assumption that 'Yes, God does exist and this is how it might be possible to explain something of what God is like.'

Theologians speak of God being **transcendent**, emphasising that God is mysterious and that it is extremely difficult for human beings to fully understand, or describe, God. Theologians also speak of God as being **immanent**, meaning that God is close to and involved with every part of creation and that human beings can experience God, even if they do not fully understand who God is or what God is like.

What does it mean to understand God as Father?

Using words like Father to describe God helps people to understand something of what God is like. Such words are analogies – a way of comparing one thing with another to help explain and make the meaning clear.

FOR DEBATE

What do you think the artist Michelangelo wanted to convey about the nature of God and his relationship to humanity in this famous painting of God creating Adam which is on the ceiling of the Sistine Chapel in Rome?

AO2 skills **ACTIVITIES**

Explore the meaning of the word 'Father'. Fathers are human beings, care for their children, are male. Can you add to this list? Now test out each of these characteristics as a description for God. Which ones do you think work and why? Which ones do not work? Why not?

RESEARCH NOTE

Look up the Lord's Prayer in Matthew 6:5–15. What does this tell you about a Christian's relationship with God the Father?

The Apostles' Creed speaks of there being one God who is the Father almighty.

- God as Father is kind, merciful and just, providing and caring for his children. The idea of God being 'almighty' suggests that God is strong and powerful.

- Good parents have a personal relationship with their children so the Apostles' Creed tells Christians that they have a personal relationship with God. The most important Christian prayer is the one that Jesus taught his disciples. It is called the Lord's Prayer and begins 'Our Father in heaven…'. You can read this prayer in Matthew 6:5–15.

One important way that Christians believe they can understand what God is like is through the teaching and life of Jesus. Jesus taught that God is a loving Father who cares for everyone.

What does it mean to believe that God is the creator?

The Apostles' Creed speaks of God being the creator of heaven and earth.

- This echoes the words of Genesis 1:1, 'In the beginning God created the heavens and the earth'. Christians believe that God is the designer, maker and sustainer of the universe.

- Different Christians have different understandings of God's role as creator. Some Christians might say 'The Bible says it was created in six days and on the seventh God rested and so that is what I believe.' Other Christians might say 'I believe that God is the creator of everything – the details of how it happened don't matter' while others might say 'I think the scientific evidence proves that the world wasn't created as it says in the Bible but that doesn't mean that God didn't create the universe.'

AO2 skills ACTIVITIES

'Saying God is like a Father is irrelevant and sexist in the 21st century – it's no wonder people don't believe in God any more.' Do you agree or disagree with this statement and why?

AO2 skills ACTIVITIES

Work in pairs to decide on at least five things that might support the idea that God created the 'heavens and the earth' and at least five things that might be against the idea that God is 'the creator'.

When you have finished share your ideas with another pair. What have you listed that is the same and what is different? As a group decide on three 'for' and three 'against' the idea that God is the creator. Then number them 1 (extremely important reason), 2 (very important reason) and 3 (important reason).

For	In support…	In support…	Opposed to…
1			
2			
3			
Against	In support…	In support…	Opposed to…
1			
2			
3			

Using the chart opposite give at least two reasons to support each statement and at least one that would argue against it.

God the Son

How is God incarnate in Jesus?

The word incarnation means 'becoming flesh,' from the Latin word *carnis* meaning 'of flesh'. It is used by Christians to describe the relationship between God the **Father** and his **Son**, Jesus. Christians believe that God took human form and lived and died in the world, and so was both human and divine.

> ### John 1:1 and 14
> *In the beginning was the Word and the Word was with God, and the Word was God...*
>
> *the Word became flesh and made his dwelling among us. We have seen his glory, the glory of the One and Only, who came from the Father, full of grace and truth.*

The verses above from the Gospel of John in the New Testament describe how God, the Creator whose words brought the world into existence, took on human form and lived among people in the person of Jesus.

The Apostles' **Creed** (see pages 6 and 7) states that Jesus is the **Christ** whose coming to Earth was promised and that Jesus is the only Son of God. This would have been regarded as blasphemous by the Jews but many Gentiles would not have found the idea of Jesus as a Son of God difficult. Some Roman emperors claimed to be divine and a son of a particular God. So, in the Creed, the use of the word 'only' is important.

The Creed emphasises that Jesus is unique as the only Son of God. It also calls him 'Lord' which shows that he is worthy of respect and obedience. It then speaks further of his special nature explaining that he was conceived of the **Holy Spirit** and born to the Virgin Mary.

The next two pages will help you to:

- understand and explain what Christians mean by the incarnation and its significance for Christians
- explore the stories of the birth, death and **resurrection** of Jesus
- express and evaluate your own views on Christian beliefs about Jesus.

MUST THINK ABOUT!

Why is the Incarnation such an important Christian belief? Write around 300 words, remembering to give reasons and try to take account of other viewpoints.

Holman Hunt's 'The Light of the World'.

How did the birth of Jesus show his divinity?

According to the Apostles' Creed Mary was a virgin when Jesus was conceived. Many Christians honour Mary for her obedience to God and the privilege given to her of being the means by which God was made known in human form. Some Christians have found belief in the **Virgin Birth** difficult and do not take it literally. Some say that the texts referring to Mary as a virgin should be translated to mean 'young woman', not necessarily a virgin.

After stating the nature of Jesus as both human and divine the Apostles' Creed affirms his suffering, crucifixion, death and burial. This is very important as a means of refuting an early Christian heresy that stated that Jesus was divine and so could not die. It was said that Simon of Cyrene, who carried Jesus' cross, took his place. The Apostles' Creed goes on to say that Jesus suffered, was crucified, died and was buried. Following this is a statement about the resurrection.

The death and resurrection of Jesus

At the age of 33, after spending three years travelling around Palestine, teaching, healing the sick and challenging the religious leaders, Jesus was arrested by Pontius Pilate, the Roman Governor of Judaea. Jesus was accused of blasphemy and was tried, found guilty and sentenced to death.

Jesus was crucified like a common criminal and was hung on a cross until he was dead. His body was placed in a tomb cut out of the rock. The entrance to the tomb was sealed with a huge stone. The tomb was guarded because there were rumours that his followers might steal the body and claim that he had risen from the dead. Two mornings later the stone had been rolled away and the tomb was empty. Several of the friends and followers of Jesus claimed to have seen him and talked with him.

Christians believe that Jesus was brought back to life by God after his crucifixion. This is a central Christian belief because it offers the promise of life after death (**eternal life**) through faith in Jesus.

The Apostles' Creed highlights the significant events in the life of Jesus as well as emphasising what Christians believe about the importance of these events and their understanding of Jesus and his relationship to God. You will need to check your own understanding of the key events in the life of Jesus in order to help you answer questions about the Creed. The activities on this page will help you to do this.

A statue of the Virgin Mary.

> **Isaiah 7.14**
> *'Therefore the Lord himself will give you a sign. Look, the young woman is with child and shall bear a son, and shall name him Immanuel.'*

 RESEARCH NOTE

Find out more about the resurrection. Try looking in Matthew 27:6–26, Mark 16:1–8; Luke 24:13–49 and John 20: 1–10. Accounts of appearances of Jesus after his death can be found in: Matthew 28:1–15; Mark 16:9–18; Luke 24:13–49 and John 20:11–29.

 **ACTIVITIES**

Write a detailed and informed response to the question 'Is Jesus the Incarnate Son of God?' Give reasons and try to include views that are different from your own as part of the evidence you draw on.

God the Holy Spirit

The next two pages will help you to:

- understand and explain what Christians believe about the **Holy Spirit**
- evaluate the evidence for the work of the Holy Spirit in the lives of Christians
- reflect on the Christian belief that the Holy Spirit is active in the world today.

Why is the Holy Spirit often represented as a dove?

I believe in the Holy Spirit

Before his **ascension** (recounted in Acts 1:8–9) Jesus promised his disciples that they would receive the power of the Holy Spirit. The ascension happened on the day of the Jewish Feast of Shavuot which celebrated the harvest and the giving of God's Law to Moses. Christians now celebrate this event as **Pentecost**, the birthday of the **Church**. The experience of the Holy Spirit that the disciples had on that day was so powerful that it changed their lives for ever. The story of this event is a dramatic one. The story below is based on the biblical account as found in Acts 2:1–41.

The fire of the Holy Spirit

After Jesus had been taken up into heaven the disciples followed his instructions and went back to Jerusalem to wait for the coming of the Holy Spirit. They waited together in an upstairs room in a house in Jerusalem with Jesus' mother, Mary, and other women who had been close friends of Jesus. They prayed together and waited nervously, not knowing what to expect. After forty days Jerusalem began to fill up with noisy crowds of people coming from all over the world to celebrate the Feast of Pentecost.

Suddenly, strange and surprising things began to happen. They heard the sound of a fierce wind tearing through the room but nothing was blown about. Then they heard the crackling of flames and saw on each other's heads flickering tongues of fire, fire that did not burn. Suddenly they felt full of energy and passion and knew that this was the Holy Spirit promised by Jesus. To their amazement they heard each other speaking in foreign languages.

 MUST THINK ABOUT!

Imagine that you could meet one of the disciples or friends of Jesus. Make a list of questions you would like to ask them about the experience of Pentecost.

They felt a great surge of power and confidence and the desire to tell everyone the good news about the life and **resurrection** of Jesus. They rushed into the streets and began to preach and to teach the crowds and were amazed that everyone was able to understand them, asking, 'Who are these men who are able to understand and speak our languages?'

Others were more cynical, saying: 'They're talking gibberish – they've been at the wine already!' With great courage Peter spoke out to the crowds: 'We are not drunk! We are followers of the teachings of **Jesus of Nazareth**. God has raised him from the dead. We have seen him alive with our own eyes. What has happened to us today is the work of the Holy Spirit.' That day 3000 people were baptised into the newly-born Christian Church as followers of Jesus.

ACTIVITIES

Research the question 'How do Christians say that the Holy Spirit works in the world today?' and present this to the class. After all the presentations, reflect on what they have taught you about the importance of the Holy Spirit for Christians today.

How does the power of the Holy Spirit work in the world?

Christians believe that the Holy Spirit has always been at work in the world. The earliest reference is in Genesis 1:2 where the Spirit hovers over the waters at creation. Christians believe this is the same spirit that spoke to and inspired the Old Testament prophets and that today it is at work in the Church, in the lives of individual Christians as well as in the world at large.

Christians believe that the power of the Holy Spirit still transforms and changes lives. It is believed that as well as giving comfort and guidance the Holy Spirit inspires, equips and gives Christians the spiritual strength to follow the teachings of Jesus.

Christians believe that the Holy Spirit gives spiritual gifts for the good of the Church and of the world, such as the ability to preach, teach and prophesy, to heal and to 'speak in tongues' just like the first disciples did.

The Holy Spirit in the world today

The Holy Spirit also helps Christians in their attempts to spread love and peace in the world. St Paul also wrote about the 'fruit of the spirit'. Christian teaching is that the Holy Spirit works through the Church and in individuals. The relationship of the Holy Spirit as part of the **Trinity** is a mysterious one. Here, Marcus, a member of a Pentecostal Church, describes his belief in the Holy Spirit.

I believe in the Holy Spirit who is the Spirit of God working miracles in the world today. In my church the pastor and elders sometimes 'lay on hands' and say a special prayer for someone who is sick. I know that some of them have been healed – that's a miracle. I believe God the Holy Spirit can do anything.

 MUST THINK ABOUT!

What connections can you find between this description of Pentecostal beliefs about the Holy Spirit and the experiences of the disciples on the first Day of Pentecost?

Sin, judgement and forgiveness

The next two pages will help you to:

- understand and explain Christian beliefs about the nature and origin of sin
- explore Christian beliefs about judgement and evaluate the impact on how Christians live
- explore Christian beliefs about **forgiveness**.

What is sin?

If you were to ask everyone in your group or class to give a definition of 'sin' they would probably say it is about doing things that are wrong, immoral or evil. For Christians, sin is something that separates humanity from God.

Christian beliefs about the origin of sin are based on a story in Genesis 3:1–24. The story, known as the Fall, tells of Adam and Eve disobeying God and falling from perfection and bringing evil into a perfect world. Their sin is described by Christians as original sin, meaning that all humans since Adam and Eve are born sinful. For most people this story is a myth which may or may not be literally true but still tells some important truths about what it means to be human.

How do Christians deal with the belief that all humans are sinful?

In the Old and New Testaments sin is seen as separating people from God. Christians believe that humans cannot cure themselves of original sin. The only way they can save themselves from the consequences of original sin is by accepting the love of God and his forgiveness and believing that Jesus died on the cross to redeem their sins. Christians demonstrate their belief by confessing their sins and being baptised. The ceremony of Christian baptism is a public commitment to turning away from sin and sinning in order to live a new life following God's will, helped by the power of the **Holy Spirit**.

Christians try to avoid sin in their lives but they recognise that, as it is in the nature of humans to give in to temptation, this is difficult. For Christians, sin is not only something you do, it can also be something you do not do. Theologians explain this as 'sins of commission' (wrong things that are done) and 'sins of omission' (good things that are not done). The Anglican Book of Common Worship includes a prayer known as 'The General Confession' which asks God for forgiveness and includes the words: 'We have left undone those things which we ought to have done; and we have done those things which we ought not to have done.'

Judgement

The Bible teaches that at death, those who trust **Christ** as their Saviour will pass into the presence of the Lord. Those who are unrepentant will pass into hell upon their death and await the last judgement of God. Those who **repent** will pass into Heaven.

Eve offering the forbidden fruit to Adam in the Garden of Eden.

AO1 skills **ACTIVITIES**

Make a list of ways in which Christians have traditionally described the story of the Fall. Discuss with the rest of the class.

AO1 skills **ACTIVITIES**

Talk about what you think sin is and what the difference is between 'sins of commission' and 'sins of omission'. Make a list of what might come under each category.

The Bible predicts many details about the future, including the next event in God's sovereign plan: the imminent return of Jesus. When Jesus returns, the dead in Jesus (those who trusted Jesus as their Saviour) will be raised from the dead and join the living in Christ to be with him in glory.

All who belong to Christ shall be made perfectly like him in body and spirit. Those who have not been saved from their sin through Christ (dead or alive) will stand before God to account for their deeds on earth. God will judge them guilty of their sin and they will justly suffer eternal condemnation in the lake of fire along with Satan and his angels.

God will make a new heaven and earth where sin no longer exists and the righteous will worship and enjoy forever the presence of their God and Saviour.

Forgiveness

Jesus taught his disciples that if they truly repented of their sins then God would forgive them and help them to live a new life. Christians believe that it is not possible to buy or earn forgiveness and **salvation** just by doing good deeds. It is only through faith in Jesus that forgiveness is received. Knowing that sins are forgiven Christians try to show how grateful they are by being generous and forgiving to other people.

When Christians experience the forgiveness of their sins and commit themselves to following Jesus they speak of 'being saved'.

 GradeStudio

AO2

QUESTION

'It is impossible to follow Jesus' teaching about forgiveness.' [12 marks]

This is an AO2 question, which means you are expected to discuss the issue raised and support different views with evidence and argument. You also have to justify a view of your own. Examiners will use four levels to assess your response. Let's look at what you need to do to move up to the higher levels.

Start by identifying the *key word* and the *key issue*. The key word is 'impossible', and the key issue is that Jesus said we should forgive again and again, even when that seems illogical and unfair.

Level 1 Start by identifying the issue and offer a point of view related to it.	Jesus said forgive seventy times seven times, meaning forever. He even followed this teaching himself when he forgave the people who crucified him. So it is possible.
Level 2 Expand on this view with further justification from another Christian teaching.	For example, the attitude of people who have worked for human rights like Martin Luther King Jr, who also always seemed able to forgive. At this level you should include another view, for example, that there are some things that are unforgivable.
Level 3 Develop alternative views and support them with evidence. Give your own view. Remember to stay focused on Christianity.	An alternative view might be that the Holocaust cannot be forgiven. Or develop the view that forgiving people means they get away with things for which they should be punished. It is easy to say sorry and expect to be forgiven. How do we know the person means it?
Level 4 Develop each argument and compare them. Explain your own view, and come to a conclusion. At this level there will be good use of technical terms such as repentance. You must refer to Christianity to achieve this level.	Comment on the value of each argument you have given and then explain your own response. For example, refer to the idea that Christians should try to forgive others, but that only God has the ability to forgive some things, as only he knows what is in the minds and hearts of people. Only he knows whether a person has really repented.

Salvation and eternal life

The next two pages will help you to:

- understand and explain Christian beliefs about **salvation** and **eternal life**
- reflect on your own ideas and responses to what you have learnt.

What is salvation?

Salvation is the mending of the relationship between God and humanity which was broken when Adam and Eve disobeyed God. Christians believe that through the death of Jesus, God has saved or redeemed humanity. They believe that, although Jesus was innocent, he died in the place of sinners. Through his death Jesus atoned for what others have done wrong.

When Christians describe Jesus as their Saviour they mean that he has saved them from sin, that he has brought them salvation. Christians sometimes describe the blood of Jesus as 'washing away sin'. In John's Gospel Jesus is called 'the Lamb of God, who takes away the sin of the world!' (John 1:29). These words are used at the celebration of the Eucharist or Holy Communion. For some Christians the bread and wine shared by Christians at the Eucharist or Holy Communion symbolise the sacrifice made by Jesus on the cross, his flesh and blood given for the salvation of the human race.

Eternal life

Christians believe that God is just, that sin is wrong, and that those who have sinned will be judged and punished. The Bible teaches that at death, those who do not trust Jesus and do not **repent** will pass into hell upon their death. Those who repent will pass into Heaven.

How does this poster show Christian belief in salvation and Jesus' sacrifice on the cross?

REMEMBER THIS

redeem/redemption To save from sin; to clear a debt.
atone/atonement To make up for something that has gone wrong, to reconcile, make as one.

Many Christians believe that there will be a Day of Judgement when the world will end and those who have not been saved from their sin through Christ, whether they are dead or alive, will stand before God to account for their deeds on earth. God will judge them guilty of their sin and they will suffer eternal condemnation in the lake of fire along with Satan and his angels.

Their punishment will be separation from God. Those who have been saved will be with God. They will live in a new heaven and earth where sin no longer exists and the righteous will worship and enjoy the presence of their God and Saviour for ever.

The everlasting life that Christians hope for is often described as eternal because it will go on for ever. The Bible has promised eternal life to Christians. This short passage from John's Gospel is one of the most frequently quoted verses in the Bible and sums up Christian belief about eternal life:

 **RESEARCH NOTE**

What key Christian beliefs about the relationship between God and humanity are contained in John 3:16?

John 3:16

For God so loved the world that he gave his one and only Son, that whoever believes in him shall not perish but have eternal life

 **FOR DEBATE**

For modern people the idea of being punished for a crime committed by someone else is unacceptable. What do you think? Make sure you justify your views.

 GradeStudio

AO1

QUESTION

What do Christians mean by salvation? **[6 marks]**

This is an AO1 question, meaning it is trying to test your knowledge and understanding. Examiners will use three levels to measure how successfully you demonstrate these skills. Let's now look at what you need to do to achieve a higher level.

The question is asking you to explain what Christians mean when they use the word salvation. It is therefore asking for more than a definition, although that is where you could start. Go on to extend the explanation and link it to other Christian beliefs that are connected to salvation, such as eternal life and the importance of living a good life.

Level 1

At this level, give a simple statement of the meaning of the word salvation to Christians. Christians believe that although God will punish people for the bad things they do, it is possible to be saved from the punishment. This is what they mean by salvation.

Level 2

To move up to this level, you need to give a deeper explanation. For example, explain how salvation may be achieved, according to some Christians, by accepting that Jesus is the son of God and believing that he was punished on the cross for the sins of mankind. This makes believers free of all sins and enables them to enter God's kingdom.

Level 3

Finally, connect this to other aspects of Christianity by explaining that although in this view, people are saved and freed from punishment just by believing in Jesus, they will also try to live a good life avoiding sin as followers of Jesus.

Frameworks for living

How do we know how we should live?

When Gordon Brown made his speech (May 2007) announcing he wanted to lead the Labour Party he spoke of his vision for Britain and of the influence that his parents had on him (his father was a Church of Scotland minister). He said 'For me, my parents were, and their inspiration still is, my moral compass. The compass has guided me through each stage of my life. They taught me the importance of integrity and decency, treating people fairly – and duty to others...'

What gives Christians guidance for living?

The Ten Commandments

The Ten Commandments are one of the oldest sets of principles for living. They are over three thousand years old. Jews and Christians believe that they were given to Moses by God and were written on stone tablets. They provide clear guidance on how God expects people to behave. You can find the Commandments in Exodus 20:1–17 and the story of how God gave them to Moses in Exodus 19.

The Ten Commandments are part of the Torah, the Jewish Scriptures. As a Jew, Jesus would have understood that the Law was the revelation of God's will for how his people were to live. He would have been brought up to follow the Ten Commandments and he referred to them in his teaching. They describe a person's responsibility to God and their responsibility to others and can be divided into religious commandments, about the way people should behave towards God, and social commandments, about how people should treat each other.

Religious commandments

1 You shall have no other gods to rival me.
2 You shall not make yourself a carved image (to worship).
3 You shall not misuse the name of God.
4 Remember the Sabbath day and keep it holy.

Social commandments

5 Honour your father and your mother.
6 You shall not commit murder.
7 You shall not commit adultery.
8 You shall not steal.
9 You shall not give false evidence.
10 You shall not envy that which belongs to someone else.

The next two pages will help you to:

- identify and understand the core teachings of Christianity
- explain how the core teachings help Christians make decisions about how they should live
- consider your own views about the relevance of those core teachings to life today
- reflect on who, or what, helps you to make decisions about what is right and what is wrong.

AO1 skills ACTIVITIES

What is a compass for? What do you think Gordon Brown means by a 'moral compass'? Who, or what, is your moral compass? Why is this? How do you decide what is right and wrong?

The two great commandments

The Gospels give a number of examples where people who were very knowledgeable about the Jewish Law, and skilled in its interpretation, posed difficult questions for Jesus to answer. In Mark 12:28–34 you can read of one such incident when a teacher of the Law asked Jesus 'Of all the commandments, which is the most important?' In his response Jesus chose the Shema, the Jewish declaration of faith found in Deuteronomy 6:4–5: 'Hear, O Israel: The Lord our God, the Lord is one. Love the Lord your God with all your heart and with all your soul and with all your strength.'

Jesus continued 'The second is this: "Love your neighbour as yourself" ', adding another commandment from Leviticus 19:18. The teacher of the Law agreed with Jesus. This conversation shows that Jesus considered the Jewish Scriptures to be the basis for the new commandments.

The Sermon on the Mount

This is a collection of blessings, parables, interpretations of the Torah and teachings about religious practices. Some of the core teachings of Christianity are found in these three chapters. It is unlikely that Jesus taught all of these ideas at the same time but when the author of the Gospel was deciding how to put his story together he decided to put these teachings of Jesus all together.

Matthew's Gospel was written for Jewish Christians and, just as Moses went to the top of Mount Sinai to receive the Torah from God, the author decided that he would have Jesus climb a mountain to teach his disciples, and the huge crowds who followed him, about some new principles for living. These teachings are sometimes called 'the new law'. They were given the title 'The Sermon on the Mount' and are found in Matthew 5–7.

Jesus giving the Sermon on the Mount.

AO1 skills **ACTIVITIES**

Read Mark 12:28–34 which says that people should love God and love others as much as they love themselves. How easy is it to put this into practice in today's world? What would the problems be? How would the world be different if everybody tried to put this into practice?

AO2 skills **ACTIVITIES**

Compare the teachings of the Beatitudes (Matthew 5:1–12) with those of the Ten Commandments. What similarities and differences can you find between them?

Welcome to the Grade Studio

GCSE is about what you can do, not what you can't do. You need to know what examiners want in your answers so you can get the best possible marks. In GCSE Religious Studies there are two things that examiners are looking for. These are called assessment objectives (AO). Questions are designed to help examiners find out how well you do in each assessment objective.

Graded examples for this topic

AO1

AO1 questions test what you know and how well you can explain and analyse things. Let's look at some AO1 questions to see what examiners are expecting you to do.

Question

Explain what Christians mean by the Trinity.   **[6 marks]**

Possible steps to answer the question: What should an answer be like and how do examiners work out what is a good response or a poor one?

Examiners use levels to measure the responses. There are three levels for AO1. A good answer will not only give a definition, it will explain in some detail what it means, how it links to other beliefs and how it affects a Christian's life. You could build an answer like this:

Student's answer

Christians believe in one God, but say that God is made up of three persons. This is said in the Creeds. The Trinity is God the Father, the Son and the Holy Spirit. All the persons are equal.

Examiner's comment

This is quite accurate but not detailed or explained. This is a weak response. It is just knowledge about the Trinity and shows little understanding and no analysis. It is more of a definition than an appropriate response to the question and therefore achieves only a Level 1.

Student's improved answer

Christians believe in one God, but say that God is made up of three persons. This idea is called the Trinity. This is said in the creeds. The Trinity is God the Father, the Son and the Holy Spirit. All the persons are equal.

Christians believe that God came to earth as Jesus and gave his life on the cross to save people from their sins. It is very difficult to understand how God could also be Jesus. The Trinity helps to explain this and also explains how God can still be experienced today. This is the Holy Spirit. The belief in the Trinity is found in the Apostles' creed which Christians recite in their worship. It is very important that people do not think that Christians believe in three Gods, the Trinity is three in one, one in three.

Examiner's comment

This response has followed the steps to answer the question. It is a good response because there is knowledge, explanation and analysis of the concept of the Trinity and appropriate use of specialist terms. This response is also a good explanation of why the Trinity is important to Christians. The reference to the creeds links the Trinity to other key beliefs of Christians. There is good analysis of how it is important because of this. The response shows a good understanding of the problem and achieves Level 3.

Question

Explain why the Ten Commandments are important for Christians.　　　　**[6 marks]**

Student's answer

The Ten Commandments are important for Christians because they are the instructions which God gave to Moses on Mount Sinai and which the Israelites were told to follow. Jesus told his followers that he had not come to change the law which God had given. So this means that Christians should also follow the Ten Commandments as well as following the teachings which Jesus gave to his followers such as those in the Sermon on the Mount.

All the Ten Commandments are important for Christians. The first four are religious commandments which tell them how they should behave towards God and the next six are social commandments which describe how they should behave towards other people.

Examiner's comment

This response has followed the steps to answer the question. It is a good response because there is knowledge, explanation and analysis of the importance of the Ten Commandments and appropriate use of specialist terms. There is good analysis of the importance and the response shows a good understanding of the question and therefore achieves Level 3.

These specimen answers provide an outline of how you could construct your response. Space does not allow us to give a full response. The examiner will be looking for more detail in your actual exam responses.

Remember and Reflect

AO1 Describe, explain and analyse, using knowledge and understanding

Find the answer on:

1 Explain, in one sentence, what each of the following key words means: *a creed b orthodox*	**PAGE 6, 7**
2 What is the Apostles' Creed and why is it important to Christians today?	**PAGE 6, 7**
3 Explain what Christians understand by the doctrine of the Trinity.	**PAGE 8**
4 Explain what Christian theologians mean by God being both transcendent and immanent.	**PAGE 10**
5 What does the Apostles' Creed say about Jesus?	**PAGE 12**
6 Explain the meaning of sin. Give examples of the difference between sins of commission and sins of omission.	**PAGE 16**
7 Recount the story of the Fall from Genesis. What does it teach Christians about sin and about the relationship between God and humanity?	**PAGE 16**
8 Explain, in one sentence, what each of the following words means: *a repentance b confession c absolution d forgiveness*	**PAGE 16, 17**
9 Outline three ways in which Christians might explain the idea of Heaven and three ways in which they might explain the idea of Hell.	**PAGE 18, 19**
10 List the Ten Commandments. Four of them are about the relationship with God and six about relationships with other people. Which are which?	**PAGE 20**
11 What are Jesus' Great Commandments and how do they relate to the Ten Commandments?	**PAGE 21**
12 Choose one passage from the Sermon on the Mount and explain what it is saying to Christians today.	**PAGE 21**

AO2 Use evidence and reasoned argument to express and evaluate personal responses, informed insights, and differing viewpoints

1. Christians must find it difficult to believe in a creator God in today's world. True or false?

2. Do you think Christian teaching as summarised in the Apostles' Creed is relevant in today's world?

3. Do you believe in life after death? Why or why not?

4. What would you say are the essential things a Christian has to believe? Why?

5. Being a Christian is not just about believing, it is about action. Respond to this statement drawing on Jesus' teaching in the Sermon on the Mount and the two Great Commandments.

6. Copy out the table, adding any other notes to the key points you think relevant and give your personal response with reasons.

Apostles' Creed	Key points	What I think and why
One God	Monotheism Trinity Co-equal and co-eternal	
Father	Creator/sustainer Transcendent and immanent	
Son	Jesus – incarnation, life, death, resurrection and ascension Forgiveness and salvation Lord and Saviour Will come again as judge	
Holy Spirit	Power of God at work in the world Miracle	
Holy catholic church and communion of saints	Universal church Unity of church v. denominational differences All Christians living and dead Spiritual relationship Special 'saints' and every Christian a 'saint'	
Forgiveness of sins, resurrection of the body, life everlasting	Through Jesus Judgement Heaven and Hell	

Topic 2: Special days and pilgrimages

The Big Picture

In this Topic you will:

- explore different ways in which Christians observe and consider the significance of special days
- explore the nature and importance of pilgrimage
- examine the role pilgrimage might play in the spiritual development of Christians.

What?

You will:

- develop your knowledge and understanding of important days in the Christian calendar, where Christians go on pilgrimage and what practices are observed when on pilgrimage
- explain the significance of these special days and how they may make a difference to a believer's life
- assess the impact of these special days on Christians and other British citizens in the 21st century
- explore the relevance of special places and journeys and why some Christians go on pilgrimage.

How?

By:

- enquiring about how different Christians observe special days
- exploring the connections between your own beliefs and those of Christians
- identifying and researching places of pilgrimage
- exploring why some Christians believe it is important to go on a pilgrimage and the relevance in the 21st century
- thinking about why journeys and places might be special to you.

Why?

Because:

- understanding about Christian pilgrimage and festivals will help you understand how Christians show their faith to God
- reflecting on these practices helps you to compare and contrast how different people show their faith, including thinking about your own ideas/beliefs.

Re-enactment of Christ carrying the cross to Golgotha.

⏰ **GET STARTED**

Think about a recent experience of visiting a special place or event and answer the following questions:

1 What did you do at this place/event?
2 Did you have a good time?
3 What feelings did you experience when you had to come home?

Special days and pilgrimages

KEY INFORMATION

- The word pilgrimage literally means a journey to a holy place or a religious journey.

- Pilgrimage is also used to describe the journey of life from birth to death that everyone is on. It can also refer to an inner journey of self-reflection where someone learns more about their character and personality and develops as a person.

- Many Christians, especially Roman Catholics, think going on a pilgrimage is a good thing to do but some Christians do not think it is a necessary part of their faith.

- Christians can go on their own but usually go as part of a big group.

- Many Christians believe that the most important place of pilgrimage is Israel (the Holy Land) because it is the country where Jesus spent his life. Jesus was born in Bethlehem, he grew up in Nazareth and he died, was buried and rose from the dead in Jerusalem.

- Other popular places of pilgrimage include: Rome, especially the Vatican because it is the home of the Pope; Lourdes, where the Virgin Mary appeared in a vision and miracles have taken place; Santiago de Compostela, Spain; Knock, Ireland; Fatima, Portugal; and Meðjugorje, Bosnia.

- There are also places of pilgrimage in Britain. These include: Walsingham, Norfolk, where the Virgin Mary appeared in a vision and a copy of Jesus' house in Nazareth was built; Canterbury, Kent; and Iona, Scotland.

- Christians celebrate many festivals and special days throughout the year.

- Advent means arrival or coming and is the period of 40 days leading up to Christmas.

- Christmas Day itself (25 December) is celebrated as the birthday of Jesus. It is followed by Boxing Day, the Feast of St Stephen, on 26 December.

- The festival of Epiphany is the 12th day of Christmas and marks the visit of the Magi to Jesus in Bethlehem.

- Shrove Tuesday, which is often marked by pancake races, is the day before the beginning of Lent.

- Ash Wednesday is the first day of Lent and, in some Churches, penitents receive the sign of the cross in ashes on their foreheads.

- Lent is a penitential period of 40 days leading up to Easter. In the last week of Lent (Holy Week) Maundy Thursday is the day when Jesus ate the Last Supper with his disciples and Good Friday recalls the day when he was crucified.

- Easter Sunday is a very important festival which celebrates the resurrection of Jesus Christ from the dead.

KEY QUESTIONS

KNOWLEDGE AND UNDERSTANDING

What sort of things do Christians do when they go on a pilgrimage to a holy place?

Why have Israel, Lourdes, Rome and Walsingham become places of pilgrimage?

Why do so many Christians think going on a pilgrimage is helpful to their faith?

ANALYSIS AND EVALUATION

Do you have to go on a pilgrimage to be a 'real' Christian?

Is it still worth going on a pilgrimage if some people doubt that the visions and miracles associated with a holy place really happened?

How is going on a pilgrimage different from going on a summer holiday?

Advent Means arrival or coming. The name given to the 40 days before Christmas.

Ash Wednesday The first day of Lent. In some Churches, penitents receive the sign of the cross in ashes on their foreheads.

Bethlehem The birthplace of Jesus.

Boxing Day The Feast of St Stephen (popularly called Boxing Day) is celebrated on 26 December.

Christmas Day Christmas Day (or Christ's Mass day) is celebrated as the birthday of Jesus.

Easter Central Christian festival which celebrates the resurrection of Jesus Christ from the dead.

epiphany Means 'to reveal'. The name of the Christian festival which celebrates the Magi visiting the infant Jesus.

incarnation The doctrine that God took human form in Jesus Christ. It is also the belief that God in Christ is active in the Church and in the world.

Jerusalem The place where Jesus died, was buried and rose from the dead.

Lent Penitential season. The 40 days leading up to Easter.

Lourdes A place of pilgrimage since 1858 when Bernadette Soubirous experienced a vision of the Virgin Mary while she was walking near a cave in Lourdes.

martyr Someone who is killed because of their beliefs.

Nazareth The place where Jesus grew up.

penance Saying 'sorry' and doing some action to show that you mean it.

pilgrimage Journey to a holy place or a religious journey.

reflection Being quiet and thoughtful, thinking deeply about things.

resurrection The rising from the dead of Jesus Christ on the third day after the crucifixion.

Rome Centre of the Roman Catholic Church.

Shrove Tuesday Celebration by Christians the day before Lent.

Walsingham A place of pilgrimage in Norfolk, England where the Virgin Mary appeared in a vision and a copy of Jesus' house in Nazareth was built.

FOR INTEREST

In the Bible the number 40 is often used to represent a period of time, for example, the Israelites spent 40 years wandering in the desert after being freed from Egypt and Jesus spent 40 days in the wilderness before he began his ministry. In this Topic you will encounter two penitential periods in the Church's year: 40 days of Advent and 40 days of Lent.

Lent

The next two pages will help you to:

- explain why **Lent** is important to Christians
- explore different ways Christians might observe Lent
- evaluate the significance of Lent for Christians.

In the United Kingdom it is traditional to race with pancakes on Shrove Tuesday.

Lent

Lent lasts 40 days, not including Sundays, and is a time of preparation for **Easter**. Lent finishes on Easter Sunday morning. It begins the day after **Shrove Tuesday** (Ash Wednesday); in some parts of the world Shrove Tuesday is called 'Fat Tuesday', in France 'Mardi Gras' and in the Caribbean 'Carnival' (Latin for 'going without meat').

In Britain, Shrove Tuesday is better known as Pancake Day. For Christians this means one last party and celebration, eating up all the nice, sweet, enjoyable things in the cupboard before beginning Lent. For some Christians this means no meat, no chocolate and cakes, no alcohol and no dairy products, for example cheese. Other Christians are more lenient and just give up eating their favourite food.

Shrove Tuesday used to be called Shriven Tuesday, an old word meaning 'to be forgiven of your sins' because Christians go to church to confess their sins to the priest and be 'shriven' or forgiven.

AO1 skills **ACTIVITIES**

Is religious observance, attending church regularly and fasting, for example, more important for a Christian than having a Christian lifestyle, forgiving and showing kindness to people? What do you think?

Why is Lent important to Christians?

Lent reminds Christians of Jesus' time of temptation and fasting (going without food) in the desert which lasted for 40 days and nights. Christians believe that by copying Jesus' example they can become better Christians. By eating less, fasting at certain times or giving up their favourite food they will have more time to focus and think about their faith, to read the Bible and pray.

They become more self-disciplined and stronger willed at resisting all types of temptation. They appreciate all the things they do have and become more aware of other people's needs. Many churches have 'hunger lunches' where Christians have soup and a bread roll and donate the money that they would have spent on lunch to charities helping in poorer countries. Other Christians give money to charities.

Lent begins on **Ash Wednesday**. In the Bible if you were really sorry for something you had done you would wear sackcloth and put ashes on your head so everyone could see you meant it. Today Roman Catholics and many members of the Church of England go to church where the priest will burn last year's Palm Sunday crosses and use the ash to put a mark on a person's forehead. There might also be a Mass or Holy Communion. The church may be decorated in purple.

AO2 skills ACTIVITIES

Looking at the statements below, can you give arguments for and against the statements? Discuss with the rest of the class.

- If you say sorry you should do it in public where other people can hear you.
- Fasting or giving something up for a period of time is a good thing to do.
- Why should I give money to a charity helping people in other countries? People in Britain need help.

On Ash Wednesday many Christians receive the sign of the cross in ashes on their foreheads as a sign of repentance at the beginning of Lent.

Holy Week and Easter

Why is Holy Week important for Christians?

Lent is a time of spiritual preparation for **Easter**. The final week of Lent is known as Holy Week. During Holy Week Christians attend special services which help them to reflect on the events leading up to the death and resurrection of Jesus. During the week they experience a wide range of emotions from deep sadness to great joy and happiness.

What happened during Holy Week?

Holy Week begins on Palm Sunday and ends at midnight on Saturday. Information about the events of Holy Week is recorded in the Gospel accounts of Matthew, Mark, Luke and John. The writers of the four Gospels were writing from different perspectives, drawing on information from different sources, and so their accounts of the events differ in some ways. It is possible to put together a timeline showing the sequence of events, drawing on these accounts.

How do Christians observe Holy Week?

Many Christians try to relive the events in this last week in the life of Jesus to try and understand his suffering, death and resurrection more deeply. The most important days are:

Palm Sunday

Christians remember the triumphant entry of Jesus into **Jerusalem**. Jesus rode on a donkey and was welcomed by cheering crowds who threw down their cloaks in the road and waved palm branches shouting 'Hosanna! Blessed is he who comes in the name of the Lord! Blessed is the King of Israel!' (John 12:13). In some towns and villages there is a procession through the streets to the church, with a donkey ridden by a child dressed as Jesus. Palm crosses are given to worshippers during the service.

The next two pages will help you to:

- recall and recount the key events in the last week of Jesus' life
- investigate and evaluate the significance of the death and resurrection of Jesus for Christians today.

AO1 skills ACTIVITIES

As you study the events of Holy Week keep a colour diary of the emotions Christians have as they go from Shrove Tuesday through Lent, to Easter Sunday. If you had to express 'feeling sad' as a colour, what would you choose? What colour is a good choice to represent 'feeling tempted'?

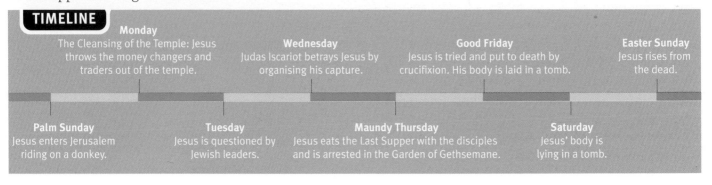

TIMELINE

Monday The Cleansing of the Temple: Jesus throws the money changers and traders out of the temple.

Wednesday Judas Iscariot betrays Jesus by organising his capture.

Good Friday Jesus is tried and put to death by crucifixion. His body is laid in a tomb.

Easter Sunday Jesus rises from the dead.

Palm Sunday Jesus enters Jerusalem riding on a donkey.

Tuesday Jesus is questioned by Jewish leaders.

Maundy Thursday Jesus eats the Last Supper with the disciples and is arrested in the Garden of Gethsemane.

Saturday Jesus' body is lying in a tomb.

Maundy Thursday

Many Christians regard this as the most solemn night of the year. They celebrate a special Eucharist service to remember the Last Supper, the last meal which Jesus ate with his Disciples before he was crucified. It was at this meal that Jesus instructed his followers to share bread and drink wine in his memory. This became the service of Holy Communion or the Eucharist which is of central importance to Christians. Jesus washed the feet of the disciples to show them how to be humble and serve each other. In some churches the priest or minister re-enacts this by washing the feet of the congregation.

Good Friday

In some places Passion Plays, which tell the story of the death of Jesus, are enacted and Christians often process through the streets carrying a large cross. Many churches hold special services to help Christians to reflect deeply on the crucifixion and death of Jesus. The service is called a 'vigil' and begins at 12 noon and lasts for three hours. Hymns about the death of Jesus may be sung, the Gospel accounts may be read and time will be spent in prayer and meditation. In Roman Catholic and some Anglican churches the congregation will make a **pilgrimage** by visiting the fourteen Stations of the Cross illustrated round the church, praying at each one.

What happened on Easter morning?

Christians believe that on the third day after Jesus' crucified body was placed in the tomb he rose from the dead and was seen by, and talked with, some of his friends and disciples. This event is called the resurrection. It is the most significant event in Christianity.

How do Christians celebrate Easter?

On Holy Saturday Christians prepare for Easter Day by cleaning the church. Many churches will have a miniature Easter garden made by the children with a model of the tomb of Jesus with the stone rolled away.

Easter Sunday is the most important day in the Christian calendar. On Easter Sunday the feelings of sadness and loss experienced during Holy Week are transformed into great joy as Christians celebrate the resurrection of Jesus. Some Christians may keep a quiet vigil in the church throughout the night.

In Roman Catholic and Orthodox churches the celebrations begin just before midnight as people go outside, leaving the church in darkness. The congregation waits outside and a great cry goes up: 'Christ is risen!' The doors of the church are opened and everyone lights lamps and candles passing them to each other, bringing light into the darkened church. A large candle (the Paschal [Easter] candle) is carried through the church, a symbol of the light of the risen Jesus shining in the darkness and the triumph of life over death. Sometimes a baby is baptised, symbolising new life. Then the first Easter Communion is celebrated.

ACTIVITIES

Can you summarise in one sentence why Easter Sunday is the most important day in the Church calendar? Go back to Topic 1 and read about the incarnation, atonement and redemption. How do these key beliefs link with the events of Holy Week and Easter?

Easter Sunday and Pentecost

The next two pages will help you to:

- understand and explain the significance of **Easter** for Christians
- explore and analyse the significance of music in Christian celebrations of Easter
- understand and explain the significance of Pentecost for Christians
- evaluate whether it is acceptable to evangelise your religion in a multi-faith society.

After the resurrection, Jesus ascended back into Heaven.

Easter Sunday

Easter Sunday is the most important day in the Christian calendar. It comes after Holy Week, a week when Christians remember with sorrow all the events leading up to the crucifixion of Jesus. On Easter Sunday morning their sadness is turned to joy as they celebrate the resurrection of Jesus from the dead.

How do Christians celebrate Easter Sunday?

- Sunrise services are held out of doors.
- Churches are decorated in white and gold.
- Candles are lit to represent Jesus as the light of the world.
- Churches are decorated with spring flowers as a symbol of new life.
- Hot cross buns and Easter eggs are eaten.
- Many Christians celebrate by attending Mass or Holy Communion.
- Special Easter hymns are sung.

AO1 skills ACTIVITIES

Music is a powerful way of expressing beliefs and emotions. Read the words from the Christian hymn below and make two lists. What beliefs are shown? What emotions can you identify? Share your ideas with the class.

66 *Thank You, Jesus,*
Thank You, Jesus
Thank You, Lord, for loving me
You went to Calvary
And there You died for me
Thank You, Lord, for loving me
You rose up from the grave
To me new life You gave
Thank You, Lord, for loving me. 99

Thank you Jesus, Alison Huntley

What happened after the resurrection?

Over the next 40 days Jesus appeared to different groups of people before ascending back into Heaven. This is celebrated on Ascension Day. The story of the ascension is in Acts 1:8–9. His last words to his disciples were that they were to wait in **Jerusalem**, but for what? The disciples and other friends of Jesus were afraid and confused. They spent the time after Jesus had ascended into Heaven in the upper room of a house in Jerusalem. They prayed and waited as Jesus had told them.

Before his ascension Jesus promised that the disciples would receive the power of the Holy Spirit. This happened on the day of the Jewish Feast of Shavuot which celebrated the harvest and the giving of God's Law to Moses. Christians now celebrate this event as Pentecost, the birthday of the Church. The experience of the Holy Spirit that the disciples had on that day was so powerful that it changed their lives forever. The story of this event is a dramatic one. It is found in the second chapter of the Acts of the Apostles.

How Christians celebrate Pentecost

Christians celebrate Pentecost as the birthday of the Church because the Holy Spirit descended in tongues of fire to the disciples. Their fear vanished. They were inspired to begin preaching and talking to people about Jesus and to encourage them to become Christians. They found that they were able to speak in strange languages and that the people who had come to Jerusalem for the festival from all over the ancient world could understand them!

That day many people were converted to Christianity and were baptised in the name of Jesus. Today Pentecost is also called Whitsun (short for 'White Sunday') because new converts to Christianity are often baptised into the Church, wearing white as a symbol of purity and a new beginning. It was also traditionally a time to buy new clothes. The story of the first Pentecost is read in churches on Whit Sunday to remind people of the roots of their faith. In some places groups from the different Christian churches come together in a procession through their towns on 'Whit walks' as a way of witnessing to their Christian faith. Christianity is a missionary religion. Jesus commanded his followers to preach the Gospel (good news) all over the world.

RESEARCH NOTE

Research the Turin shroud. Do you think this is evidence for Jesus rising from the dead? Would there be Christianity if Jesus didn't rise from the dead?

AO2 skills ACTIVITIES

How acceptable do you think it is for Christians or members of other religions actively to evangelise (try to convert others to their faith) in Britain's multi-faith society?

Explain how you think Christians or members of other religions would respond to this?

Advent

The importance of Advent

Advent means 'coming'. It begins four Sundays before Christmas and is a time when Christians reflect on and prepare themselves spiritually for the coming of Christmas. The Bible readings in churches during that period refer to Jesus coming as a baby and also to his promised return at the end of time to judge everyone. This is called the Second Coming.

Some churches hold special carol services with Bible readings and carols that tell the whole story of Christian belief about Jesus. These services start with the story of Adam and Eve and the Fall, from Genesis chapter 3, and end with the passage from St John's Gospel, which describes the incarnation, how the Word of God was 'made flesh' in the coming of Jesus, John 1:1–14. The most well known of these Advent carol services is held in King's College Chapel, Cambridge, on Christmas Eve, and is broadcast all over the world.

> ### John 1:1–5, 10–14
>
> *In the beginning was the Word, and the Word was with God, and the Word was God. He was with God in the beginning.*
>
> *Through him all things were made; without him nothing was made that has been made. In him was life, and that life was the light of men. The light shines in the darkness, but the darkness has not understood it…*
>
> *He was in the world, and though the world was made through him, the world did not recognize him. He came to that which was his own, but his own did not receive him. Yet to all who received him, to those who believed in his name, he gave the right to become children of God-children born not of natural descent, nor of human decision or a husband's will, but born of God.*
>
> *The Word became flesh and made his dwelling among us. We have seen his glory, the glory of the One and Only, who came from the Father, full of grace and truth.*

Many churches put on Nativity plays and there is often a model of the scene at the manger, showing the birth of Jesus, set up in the church. Christians often have Advent calendars and Advent candles in their homes to remind them of the 'countdown' to the coming of Christmas.

Churches sometimes have an Advent wreath made of holly and other evergreen leaves. The holly leaves represent the crown of thorns and the red berries Jesus' blood. There are four red candles to represent the four weeks of Advent. Some churches have adopted the Scandinavian custom of Christingle when every child is given an orange and a candle with a red ribbon tied around it to symbolise the blood of Jesus and God's love encircling the world.

The next two pages will help you to:

- understand and explain why **Advent** is important to Christians
- analyse how and why Christians and non-religious people celebrate Advent.

 **ACTIVITIES**

What is the connection between the story of the Fall in Genesis and the coming of Jesus? Discuss with the rest of the class.

 MUST THINK ABOUT!

Why do Christians have symbols that remind them of the death of Jesus when they are preparing to celebrate his birth?

How do Christians and non-religious people prepare for Christmas?

Create a table like this in your notes:

Christians	Non-religious people

Read the list of preparations people make for Christmas and decide which things are likely to be done by Christians, by non-religious people or by either, and write them into the correct column in your notes.

- Some churches have purple decorations on walls and altars. Purple is the colour of preparation and penitence (being sorry).
- The vicar wears purple vestments (robes).
- Advent calendars.
- Buying presents.
- Light an Advent crown or wreath on each Sunday in Advent.
- Light candles to remind people that Jesus is 'The Light of the World'.
- Read Old Testament prophecies about Jesus' coming.
- Writing Christmas cards.
- Nativity plays.
- Fasting.
- Praying, especially asking for forgiveness.
- Going to parties.
- Take time out to reflect on personal values, commitment to God.
- Eating Christmas pudding and turkey.
- Visiting friends and family.
- Candlelit carol services.
- Carol singing to raise money for charities.
- Going to Mass or Holy Communion on Christmas Eve.
- Putting up Christmas trees and decorations.
- Hanging out a stocking for Father Christmas.

The information about the Fall and the **incarnation** in Topic 1 will be useful in helping you to understand the significance of Advent and Christmas.

Isaiah 9:6

For to us a child is born,
to us a son is given,
and the government will be on his shoulders.
And he will be called
Wonderful Counsellor, Mighty God,
Everlasting Father, Prince of Peace.

Christmas and Epiphany

The next two pages will help you to:

- understand and explain how and why Christians celebrate Christmas and **Epiphany**
- analyse the symbolism of the celebration of Epiphany
- reflect on and evaluate whether Christmas has become too commercialised and its religious significance forgotten.

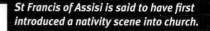
St Francis of Assisi is said to have first introduced a nativity scene into church.

Christmas

Christmas Day (originally Christ's Mass day) is celebrated as the birthday of Jesus. As this is a celebration many churches will be decorated in white and gold. Most Christians celebrate on 25 December but some Orthodox Christians celebrate on 7 January. The Bible does not actually give the date that Jesus was born. The writers of the Gospels were more concerned to explain the significance and importance of Jesus' birth. Scholars think Christians adapted a Roman festival that was celebrated on 25 December.

The Feast of St Stephen (popularly called **Boxing Day**) is celebrated on 26 December. Stephen was the first Christian **martyr**. You can read his story in the Bible in Acts 6–7.

 RESEARCH NOTE

Find out why the Orthodox Church celebrates festivals on different dates from the Catholic and Anglican Churches. You could begin by looking up the Julian calendar.

What is the meaning of Christmas for Christians?

More people attend midnight Mass on Christmas Eve than at any other time of the year. On Christmas morning many Christians go to church and many churches have special Christmas family services.

Many Christians try to express the spirit of Christmas by helping others. They may spend time helping to provide a meal for elderly or homeless people. Churches may organise charity fundraising events. They do this because they believe that they are following the teaching of Jesus to care for people who are in need. The story of the birth of Jesus is set in a stable. Mary and Joseph had nowhere to stay for the night and Jesus was born amongst the animals and placed in a manger. The first people who came to visit him were ordinary shepherds from the hillsides near **Bethlehem**.

Jesus emphasised in his parable of the sheep and the goats in Matthew 25 that, at the final judgement, people will be judged by how much they have cared for people in need.

Epiphany

Epiphany takes place on 6 January and marks the end of the Christmas festival. It is also known as 'Twelfth Night' when, according to tradition, all Christmas trees and decorations should be taken down.

Epiphany is a Greek word which means 'displaying' or 'revealing'. It is seen by Christians as a time to celebrate the occasions when the identity of Jesus as Saviour was made known. There are three events remembered and celebrated at this festival.

Most churches celebrate the showing of the baby Jesus to the wise men (Matthew 2:1–12). The Orthodox Churches, in particular, celebrate the first miracle performed by Jesus when he transformed water into wine (John 2:1–11) and the baptism of Jesus in the River Jordan by John the Baptist (Matthew 3:13–17). On each of these occasions Jesus was marked out as special in some way.

During Epiphany Christians remember and celebrate the Magi (wise men) visiting Jesus with their gifts. The wise men came from the east. They were the first Gentiles (people who are not Jewish) to visit Jesus and the true identity and purpose of Jesus' life was revealed to them. The symbolism of the gifts they brought (gold, frankincense and myrrh) are understood by Christians to be:

- gold to show the kingship of Jesus
- frankincense representing priesthood
- myrrh for suffering and death.

Traditional stories are told about the Magi and they are named as Balthasar, king of Arabia, Melchior, king of Persia, and Caspar, king of India. Christians believe the story of the visit of the wise men is showing that followers of Jesus can come from any nationality.

Not all Christians celebrate Epiphany but those who do might attend Mass or Holy Communion, read relevant Bible passages and decorate the church in white, recognising the importance of Jesus.

AO1 skills ACTIVITIES

Read the three Epiphany stories from the gospels which reveal that Jesus is special (Matthew 2:1–12, Matthew 3:13–17 and John 2:1–11). What is each story showing about the special qualities of Jesus?

RESEARCH NOTE

Find out about the work of Crisis, a charity which provides food and care for more than 2000 homeless people. At Christmas they need 6500 volunteers to help with their work.

AO2 skills ACTIVITIES

Look up T.S. Eliot's poem 'The Journey of the Magi'. You may find some of it difficult but it is worth exploring to see how the poet develops the story of the visit of the wise men to Jesus. What symbolism does he use? How does he link the birth of Jesus with his death?

Sundays and Saints' Days

The next two pages will help you to:

- explain why Christians consider Sunday to be a special day
- express views on what are appropriate ways to spend Sundays
- evaluate whether a belief in saints is helpful to someone living a Christian life.

Why is Sunday special?

The name Sunday comes from the Romans and Greeks calling the first day of the week after the Sun god. Many Christians refer to Sunday as the Lord's Day. Sunday is the first day of the week and symbolises the new beginning and new life Jesus offers to people when they become Christians. Jesus rose from the dead on the first day of the week which is now called Sunday.

The story of the creation in the book of Genesis tells how God created the world in six days and rested on the seventh day. The seventh day, of course, is actually Saturday, and this is the Sabbath, the day which Jews celebrate in obedience to the commandment in Exodus 20.

How do Christians celebrate on Sundays?

The early Christians met together to break bread on the first day of the week, recalling the day of the resurrection. Acts 20:7 refers to this practice. Most Christians believe Sunday is a day for attending church services. If people cannot attend church then often they will spend time reading their Bible, praying, listening to a church service on the radio or watching religious programmes on television, for example *Songs of Praise*. Sometimes churches will hold a service at a residential home for the elderly or in a hospital on a Sunday afternoon for people to attend.

Besides attending church what else should you do on Sundays? This is where different Christian churches have different ideas.

- Roman Catholic Christians think the day should be spent relaxing, playing sport, developing your hobbies and interests and enjoying yourself.
- Most other Christians think you can do what you like on this day but try and keep it different from the other days of the week. One easy way of doing this is not to work.
- Some Christians take Sunday as a day of complete rest because it is instructed in the Ten Commandments.

Saints' days

Roman Catholic, Orthodox and many Church of England Christians use the word saint to describe a Christian who has led a particularly good and holy life, giving other people an insight into God's character. A saint is also a good role model for other Christians to imitate in their lives. Some Christians, particularly Roman Catholics, believe that

ACTIVITIES

Eric Liddell was a sportsman who went to the 1924 Olympic Games in Paris representing Britain. He refused to run the qualifying heat in his best sporting event, the 100 metres, because it fell on a Sunday. What happened next? Check it out by researching on the Internet or by watching the film '*Chariots of Fire*' which tells the story.

Exodus 20:8–10

Remember the Sabbath day by keeping it holy. Six days you shall labour and do all your work, but the seventh day is a Sabbath to the Lord your God. On it you shall not do any work, neither you, nor your son or daughter, nor your manservant or maidservant, nor your animals, nor the alien within your gates. For in six days the Lord made the heavens and the earth, the sea, and all that is in them, but he rested on the seventh day. Therefore the Lord blessed the Sabbath day and made it holy.

saints can also be prayed to and asked to intercede (speak on behalf of someone) to God. The Apostles' Creed refers to the communion of saints. The Bible calls all Christians saints because they have been sanctified, or made holy (different from the world), when they became Christians.

A saint's day is an opportunity to learn about the life of the saint being remembered.

In the Orthodox Church they use icons of saints. This is a very special type of art called iconography. They are paintings but drawn in a way that shows something about their personality, for example saints are always shown with small mouths. Why do you think this is? If saints are role models, what should a Christian be learning? If you study art you might like to talk to your art teacher for more information.

All Saints' Day

All Saints' Day is on the first Sunday in November and is an opportunity to remember all saints. This used to be celebrated by many people in Britain as a time to remember their relatives and loved ones, for example by visiting their graves to leave flowers. It used to be called All Hallows Day. Today few people remember this day but they do know 31 October, Hallowe'en or All Hallows Eve. This is an old festival from pre-Christian times in Britain which marked the end of the harvest.

RESEARCH NOTE

Who are the patron Saints of England, Ireland, Scotland and Wales? Many local churches will be named after saints. Name as many local churches as you can. If you get stuck look in the local telephone directory. Find out about the life of one of the saints and why they were made a saint.

ACTIVITIES

Other Christians do not agree with this belief in saints. Some say you might end up worshipping the saint instead of God and this would be breaking the Ten Commandments. One of these says 'You shall have no other gods before me.' What do you think? Which Christian view do you agree with and why?

GradeStudio

AO1

QUESTION

Why is Sunday special for Christians? **[6 marks]**

This is an AO1 question, meaning it is trying to test your knowledge and understanding. Examiners will use three levels to measure how successfully you demonstrate these skills. Let's now look at what you need to do to achieve a higher level.

Although the word 'explain' is not in the question, that is what you are being asked to do. To achieve the highest level, you should try to give three good reasons for Sunday being special.

Level 1

Start with a key point such as Sunday is special for Christians because it is the day Jesus rose from the dead.

Level 2

Develop the first point by saying how the resurrection is central to Christian belief. Suggest another reason for example, that Christianity developed from Judaism. Jews are required to rest on the seventh (Sabbath) day as God did at the end of creating the world. The idea of a special day set aside for worship and rest naturally followed into Christianity, with the change of the day from Saturday to Sunday.

Level 3

Develop these reasons by adding, for example, that Sunday is a day set aside for worship and recharging of the spiritual batteries, or comment on the importance to some Christians of the strict observance of Sunday as a day of rest.

Places of pilgrimage: Israel

The next two pages will help you to:

- explore why Israel is a place of **pilgrimage**
- explain the reasons why many Christians find going on a pilgrimage helpful to their faith
- reflect on and evaluate whether pilgrimage is an essential part of being a Christian.

Pilgrimage to Israel

Below Claire, a Christian, talks about her experiences when she went on a pilgrimage to Israel.

Why did you want to go?

The opportunity of going to Israel was too important to pass up even though it meant I couldn't afford to have a new bathroom. The thought of actually going to Israel and walking in the footsteps of Jesus, seeing where he performed miracles, told parables... amazing... It just brought all the stories in the Bible alive in a way that reading them at home or in church doesn't. The vicar told us that Jesus got his ideas for parables from things he saw around him so things just made more sense... farmers still sow seeds like Jesus described in the Parable of the Sower.

Where did you go? Was it what you expected? What was it like? What did you do?

In Bethlehem we went to the Church of the Nativity. This was a cave – apparently they were used as stables in Jesus' time but it has a church built over it and is very decorated with lots of incense and candles. A hole in the ground marks the spot where Jesus was actually born. I liked the doorway into the church – it was very low so you had to bend over to get in. This was done so everyone shows respect.

In Nazareth you can't see the house that Jesus grew up in but you can go to the Church of the Annunciation where the angel Gabriel appeared to Mary and told her she was going to have baby Jesus.

Jerusalem had the biggest impact on me as we re-traced Jesus' final days from Maundy Thursday through to Easter Sunday. We visited the room where Jesus and his disciples celebrated the Last Supper, held a communion service there and then went to the Garden of Gethsemane where Jesus was betrayed by Judas and arrested. Some of the olive trees there are said to be 2000 years old and I wondered what they would say about events that night if trees could talk? The vicar read the relevant passages from the Bible and being there made it easy to imagine the feelings and emotions of Jesus that night – the hurt at being betrayed by his friends, the pain and fear at knowing how horrible his death was going to be. It made me really appreciate Jesus' sacrifice and death so God

Significant holy sites in Israel,
(a) Church of the Nativity,
(b) Church of the Annunciation,
(c) Garden of Gethsemane,
(d) Church of the Holy Sepulchre.

would forgive my sins. The vicar was quite graphic in his description of how someone was crucified.

It got a bit confusing then – there are two different sites for Calvary or Golgotha, the place of the skull, where Jesus was crucified and two different sites for Jesus' tomb. Most Protestants, like me, think it happened at the hill which looks like a skull because that's how the Bible describes it and the Bible is God's Word. Nearby is a garden, with a tomb cut into the rock, with a groove for a stone to be rolled along, across its entrance. It was very quiet and peaceful, just like I imagined it to be. We had an open air service here to celebrate Jesus' resurrection, singing joyful hymns and choruses.

Most other Christians think Jesus' crucifixion and tomb are inside the Church of the Holy Sepulchre. It looks different from the outside because it has two domes – under the big dome is Jesus' tomb and the smaller dome has the rock where Jesus was crucified. Roman Catholics walk the Via Dolorosa, the route Jesus took to his death before reaching the Church. This was incredibly moving for many Christians as some were crying. There were too many people inside so it was difficult to sense the atmosphere but I suppose it taught me patience! It's confusing for me because my brain says this is most likely to be the place where Jesus' death and burial took place. Scholars say there is historical evidence for this being the place but my heart says it's the other place. It's really hard to imagine with a great big church built over the top!

ACTIVITIES

Read the interview with Claire and pick out the following information and record into your notes. Use a different coloured pen for each question.

- What were Claire's emotions and feelings?
- What are the reasons Claire went on pilgrimage to Israel?
- Do you think pilgrimage is an essential part of being a Christian? Why?

GradeStudio

AO1

The first three parts of each question, a to c, will be point marked as they will mainly ask for factual information. You need to understand the wording examiners use, respond clearly and concisely and choose good examples of knowledge.

Tip: always look carefully at the number of marks available! This should guide you as to how much you need to write.

QUESTION

State one place of pilgrimage for Christians. **[1 mark]**

'State' is the word examiners use when they want you to give a clear factual response. You have to know about one of the places given in the specification. An acceptable response would be simply, Israel.

QUESTION

State two things which a Christian might do to prepare for a pilgrimage to this place. **[2 marks]**

Remember this is a Religious Studies course so the examiner is expecting the response to be about religious activities, not about remembering to pack the sun cream!

Student's response

Pray to get the pilgrim into the right frame of mind for the journey and the visit. Attend a special Mass, or church service, for the sick who are making the pilgrimage.

QUESTION

Describe three activities which occur at this place of pilgrimage. **[3 marks]**

If possible select three religious activities that are specific to this place rather than general activities that could take place at any religious site. A good response would read:

Student's response

Pilgrims will visit Jerusalem where Jesus was betrayed by Judas, was crucified and rose from the dead. They can visit the Garden of Gethsemane, the place of the skull, and listen to relevant passages being read from the Bible. They may also attend mass.

Places of Pilgrimage:
Lourdes, Rome and Walsingham

The next two pages will help you to:

- explain why **Lourdes**, **Rome** and **Walsingham** are places of **pilgrimage**
- examine the different places of pilgrimage in Christianity
- evaluate whether pilgrimage is an essential part of being a Christian.

Why is Lourdes a place of pilgrimage?

Lourdes has been a place of pilgrimage since 1858. Bernadette Soubirous was 14 years old when she experienced a vision of a woman dressed in white wearing a blue sash and holding a rosary while she was walking near a cave in Lourdes. The woman revealed herself to be the Virgin Mary. This happened 18 times. No one other than Bernadette saw or heard anything.

Bernadette was told that people would be healed if they visited the spring that miraculously appeared and that she was to ask the local priest to build a church at the site and hold regular processions. At first people did not believe her, even the local priest. She was even interrogated by the police.

They only believed her after the woman in white told her to call her 'Mary of the Immaculate Conception'. The local priest believed her.

A church was built, a marble statue was put in the cave and people coming there began to drink the water and be healed. Bernadette herself became a nun.

Rome

This is an important place of pilgrimage for several reasons.
- Legend says that Peter was crucified in Rome and that he is buried under the altar of St Peter's Basilica.

Bernadette Soubirous.

FOR INTEREST

What are the benefits of going on a pilgrimage to Lourdes?
- Feel closer to God as it is a holy place because of Bernadette's visions
- Strengthens relationships with other Christians and everyone feels part of a big family
- Helps to put life into perspective – material possessions are not as important
- Strengthens faith and helps people grow into better Christians e.g. more patient, understanding of others
- Some people are physically cured from serious illnesses
- Other people have spiritual healing e.g. feel God has forgiven their sins, no longer feel guilty or hurt about a situation
- Putting the effort and money into going shows commitment to God
- It's a way of giving thanks to God

Pope Benedict XVI blessing people in St Paul's Square, The Vatican City.

- There is a legend that St Paul was put to death in Rome during the persecutions of Christians in 64 CE. Because he was a Roman citizen he would have been beheaded outside the walls of the city. His body is thought to have been buried under the church of St Paul outside the walls. The original church was replaced in 386 and rebuilt in 1823. There is a monastery, built on the traditional site of his death, three miles outside Rome.
- The Pope, the head of the Roman Catholic Church, lives in the Vatican City which is an independent state in the centre of Rome.
- It has always been a centre of Christianity from the earliest days of Christianity, even when it was dangerous to be a Christian and people risked being killed because of their faith.

Walsingham

England's Nazareth is the alternative name given to Walsingham in Norfolk, England's most visited place of pilgrimage. In 1061 a woman called Richeldis de Faverches had a vision of the Virgin Mary who showed her Jesus' home in **Nazareth** or The Holy House of the Annunciation. A replica house was built in Walsingham for pilgrims to visit because it was so difficult to make the journey to Israel. Today 500,000 pilgrims a year visit. Walsingham is very popular with both Roman Catholic and Protestant Christians.

Some Christians will walk from their home town or city and many others will walk the last mile to the site barefoot as a sign of humility and **penance**. When there Christians will reflect on Jesus' incarnation, take part in church services, and pray for themselves and for the world.

RESEARCH NOTE

Find out five key facts about Peter and Paul and why they are considered such important Christians.

AO2 skills ACTIVITIES

Walsingham has been voted England's favourite spiritual place by radio listeners. Conduct a class survey asking people of different ages and backgrounds, religious or non-religious, where their favourite spiritual place is. Collate the results using pie charts or bar graphs. What conclusions can you make? Do you have to be religious to be spiritual? How would you define the word 'spiritual'?

GradeStudio

AO2

QUESTION

'Every Christian must go on a pilgrimage.' **[12 marks]**

This is an AO2 question, which means you are expected to discuss the issue raised and support different views with evidence and argument. You also have to justify a view of your own. Examiners will use four levels to assess your response. Let's look at what you need to do to move up to the higher levels.

First of all identify the issue in the statement. The key words are *every* and *must*. Then consider views about the issues.

Level 1
Introduce your response by explaining why pilgrimage is important to some Christians, for example it shows devotion, strength of faith, sacrifice; it gives the opportunity to share an experience with other pilgrims and gain benefit from the place visited.

Level 2
To move up a level, develop this into the view that pilgrimage is of such great value that every Christian will benefit from it and must take part. Mention an alternative view such as that modern lifestyles and work patterns make pilgrimage difficult.

Level 3
Now try to bring in other ideas such as not all Christians believe in the significance of the places of pilgrimage or that some Christians regard pilgrimage as unnecessary. Support the views with evidence and develop each argument. Give your own view.

Level 4
Finally, explain your own view and support it with reference to Christianity. Refer to the other arguments and evaluate them to come to a conclusion. For example, not everyone can go on a pilgrimage and it is not something Jesus ever commanded Christians to do; it may be something to aspire to but it is not an essential part of being a Christian; other things such as giving to the poor, living a good life, and bringing up your family in the faith are just as important.

GradeStudio

Welcome to the Grade Studio

This unit is all about how Christianity comes alive for people through celebrations, by making a special effort at certain points in the year and also by making special journeys. In this Grade Studio we will look at how you can build really good responses to AO1 and AO2 questions to ensure you give the examiner all the evidence needed to reward you with Level 3.

Examiners will be keen to find out what you know about the special days and pilgrimage, but they also want you to show that you understand how these relate to the beliefs of Christians and how they are important to individual Christians and to the Christian community.

Graded examples for this topic

AO1

In the first three parts of a question you might have been asked to choose a place of pilgrimage and describe the sort of things Christians would do when they visit the place. The fourth part (d) of the question could be like this:

Question

Explain why Lourdes is important for Christians.   **[6 marks]**

This question, which is worth 6 marks, is asking you to explain and analyse why Lourdes is important. Your answer will be based on the knowledge you have about the place of pilgrimage, so make sure you know all about **one** of the places mentioned in the specification.

> The key word in the question is important. However, there are different ways in which the place could be important – because of the history of the place, an event that took place there, the sort of things that go on there now and the effect the visit to it could have on the pilgrim.

Student's answer

A visit to Lourdes is important because of Bernadette's vision, the source of water and the possibility of being healed physically as well as spiritually. A visit to Lourdes is important because of reasons which could apply to any pilgrimage. This could include the journey being a metaphor for the journey of life with all its difficulties and joys, the companionship which comes from journeying with other pilgrims or the spiritual importance and benefit of worshipping with others at a special place.

Pilgrimage requires sacrifice and strength of faith and also shows devotion to God in a way that other acts of worship do not.

Examiner's comment

In the exam, the response would be more developed but this could be a good response achieving Level 3 because it focuses first of all on specific information about a visit to Lourdes and secondly then includes significant points about pilgrimage in general. There is scope for analysis in the last point about how pilgrimage is important because it enables the pilgrim to show devotion to God in a special way.

Remember: responses to parts d and e of each question will be marked according to Levels of Response. For AO1, there are three levels. A good response to part d will be well organised, contain relevant knowledge and have a full, well developed explanation. If required, you should analyse the topic, which means you might make a comparison between two aspects of the topic.

Be careful: A general response which could apply to almost any place of pilgrimage will get some marks, but could not get full marks. It might only achieve Level 1 or at most the bottom marks for Level 2. Because the question refers to 'Lourdes', the highest level will be given to answers which explain why the special features of this place are important, but of course it is important for general as well as specific reasons.

AO2

Remember: AO2 is about examining points of view and expressing your own views, using evidence and argument to support them. Examiners will use levels of response to judge the quality of your work and the best responses will have plenty of evidence to support different points of view. For AO2 there are four levels of response and for the top level the response will have a personal view supported by evidence and argument.

Here are some examples of topics which you might be asked to comment on and explain views about:

- Whether the special days are any different from holidays and non-religious days off such as New Year.
- Whether all Christians should go on a pilgrimage to be 'real' Christians.
- Whether one festival or special day is more important to Christians than another.

Do some research about each of these topics and, using a table format such as the one below, note down different views people might hold on these issues. Develop your own view and collect evidence and develop arguments to support it. Use this table format as a way of planning much more detailed notes. The plan will need to be reviewed once you have developed your notes, but it will be a very useful revision guide at the end of the course.

Here is a brief example which you could build on:

Question

Christmas is more important to Christians than Easter.   [12 marks]

Student's answer

Level 1
Christmas is the more important festival because it is more popular and because it celebrates the birth of Jesus the saviour.

Level 2
Easter is more important because it celebrates the event of the resurrection of Jesus which is the key belief of Christians.

Level 3
I think that neither is more important. They are equally significant to Christians but are celebrated differently. Although Christmas is more popular and celebrated more by the public, this does not make it more important to Christians. They are equally significant and the faith could not exist without either event.

Examiner's comment

In your own work you need to be much more detailed to ensure you achieve the level suggested, but if you use this structure you will be guided to develop good responses.

Level 4 could be achieved if the views, including an appropriate personal response, are well argued and supported by evidence.

AO2 questions are worth 50% of the marks for each question, so you must practise expressing other people's views and develop your own view and support it with evidence.

You also need to practise holding back from expressing your own view until you have explained and made comments about the views of others.

Often candidates lose marks because they get too wound up about their own view, forgetting to express other views. This limits what might otherwise be a good response to Level 1 or Level 2.

These specimen answers provide an outline of how you could construct your response. Space does not allow us to give a full response. The examiner will be looking for more detail in your actual exam responses.

Remember and Reflect

AO1 Describe, explain and analyse, using knowledge and understanding

Find the answer on:

1 What do these words mean:
   a *Advent*   b *Epiphany*   c *incarnation*   d *resurrection*

> **PAGE 29**

2 For each festival state which event in Jesus' life is being celebrated:
   a *Christmas*   b *Epiphany*   c *Lent*   d *Good Friday*
   e *Easter Sunday*   f *Ascension*

> **PAGE 29**

3 Explain five ways a Christian will prepare for Advent. How is this different from non-religious ways of preparing for Advent?

> **PAGE 36, 37**

4 What do Christians think the real meaning of Christmas is?

> **PAGE 39**

5 What is the time of preparation for Easter called? What preparations will Christians make and why?

> **PAGE 32**

6 Describe, in as much detail as you can, what happened in Jesus' life on:
   a *Palm Sunday*   b *Maundy Thursday*   c *Good Friday*

> **PAGE 32, 33**

7 Explain what Christians believe about the significance of Jesus' death and resurrection.

> **PAGE 34, 35**

8 How do Christians celebrate Easter?

> **PAGE 34**

9 How is Pentecost celebrated by Christians?

> **PAGE 35**

10 What is the special day of the week for Christians? Explain the different ways Christians spend the day.

> **PAGE 40**

11 Who or what is a saint? Name one. Why do some Christians think remembering a saint is a good thing to do?

> **PAGE 40, 41**

12 Give three different meanings of the word 'pilgrimage'.

> **PAGE 44**

13 Name four places Christians might visit on pilgrimage.

> **PAGE 44**

14 Explain how Lourdes became a place of pilgrimage.

> **PAGE 44**

15 What activities do Christians take part in when at Lourdes?

> **PAGE 44**

16 Create a list of all the benefits Christians have from going on a pilgrimage to Lourdes.

> **PAGE 44**

17 Now, add to this list any different benefits that Christians have found from visiting:
   a *Israel*   b *Walsingham*   c *Rome*

> **PAGE 42, 43, 44, 45**

18 Explain why Israel is a place of pilgrimage for Christians.

> **PAGE 42**

19 Explain why **either** Walsingham **or** Rome is a place of pilgrimage.

> **PAGE 44, 45**

20 List four other ways (not including festivals or pilgrimage) that a person can show that they are a Christian.

> **PAGE 42**

AO2 Use evidence and reasoned argument to express and evaluate personal responses, informed insights, and differing viewpoints

Answer the following, giving as much detail as possible. You should give at least three reasons to support your response and also show that you have taken into account opposite opinions.

1 Which festival is more important to Christians – Christmas or Easter?

2 'Christmas celebrations should be banned.' How far do you agree?

3 'Fasting or giving something up for Lent is a good thing to do.' How far do you agree?

4 'The real meaning of Easter has been forgotten amongst all the chocolate Easter eggs.' True or false?

5 The government wants to extend the opening hours of shops on Sundays. What do you think? What might a Christian say? What might someone from another religion say?

6 'A pilgrimage is just another name for a holiday.' How far do you agree?

7 If you had to choose one destination for a pilgrimage, which one would you choose – Lourdes or Israel?

8 'To show everyone you are serious about being a Christian you have to go on a pilgrimage.' True or false?

9 'If you don't know if the visions happened, which spot Jesus was crucified on or if a saint really is buried there then pilgrimages are just making money from gullible people.' How far do you agree?

10 Going on a pilgrimage or putting Jesus' teaching in the Sermon on the Mount into practice. Which one is more important? Why?

Pilgrims visiting the ruins of the original shrine of Our Lady of Walsingham.

Topic 3: Major divisions and interpretations

The Big Picture

In this Topic you will:

- analyse the main similarities and differences between: Roman Catholic, Orthodox and Protestant Christianity
- consider why there are different denominations in Christianity and explore how Christianity is practised in different parts of the world and how these differences might affect the lifestyles and outlooks of Christians in the modern world
- explore the nature, growth and effects of ecumenism with reference to:
  - the World Council of Churches
  - shared worship
  - shared churches
  - combined charitable activities
  - ecumenical communities – Taizé, Iona, Corrymeela.

What?

You will:

- develop your knowledge and understanding of the beliefs, organisation, sources of authority, worship and practices of different denominations
- consider ways in which different denominations can work together
- explore the challenges facing Christian denominations in the 21st century and evaluate how the denominations respond to these challenges.

Why?

Because:

- it is important to understand the history of Christianity in Britain and have some insight into how Christianity is practised as a worldwide religion.

How?

By:

- investigating the similarities and differences between different Christian denominations
- researching different ways in which Churches work together
- exploring the challenges facing Christian denominations and evaluating how successful their responses are.

Interior of an Orthodox Church.

GET STARTED

In pairs, on a piece of paper, create two headings. One is the name of your school, the other a different school in your area. In what ways are the schools similar and different? Do you have more in common or more differences?

Major divisions and interpretations

KEY INFORMATION

- There are many different Christian Churches or **denominations**, which means 'types of' Church.

- The biggest denominations in Christianity are Roman Catholic, Orthodox and Protestant.

- There are many different types of Protestants.

- Christians are not just found in Britain. Christianity is the world's biggest religion and anywhere you go in the world you will find different Churches.

- Christian denominations have much in common; for example they accept the beliefs found in the Apostles' Creed (see Topic 1); they use the Bible for help and guidance on how to live as a Christian (see Topic 6) and practise Jesus' example of loving and caring for other people.

- But they have differences and disagree on other things; for example, how should God be worshipped? How important is a church building? Do churches need priests? Can women be priests? Attitudes on moral issues can also cause differences; for example what methods of contraception are acceptable? What sources of authority should Christians use when they want advice?

- In the past hundred years the different denominations in Christianity have begun to talk to each other to see if they can agree on issues they disagree over.

- Some Christians have gone further and created denomination-free communities that any Christian can attend, for example Taizé, Iona and Corrymeela.

- Other denominations have been led to work together because they have fewer people coming to church and cannot afford to run their own church building. They often share a church building with another denomination. This is called **ecumenism**.

KEY QUESTIONS

KNOWLEDGE AND UNDERSTANDING
Why are there different Christian denominations?

What are the differences and similarities between different denominations?

How are the denominations responding to face the challenges of life in the 21st century?

In what ways are different churches working together?

ANALYSIS AND EVALUATION
Will the denominations be able to work through their differences and unite?

Christians have more denominations than any other religion – what are the advantages and disadvantages of having many denominations?

Do the denominations have more in common than they have differences?

How successful has the ecumenical movement been in encouraging churches to work together?

Anglican Church Churches in full communion with the Archdiocese of Canterbury. Their origins and traditions are linked to the Church of England, and they are part of the Anglican Communion.

apostolic succession The doctrine (church teaching) connecting the Church to the original Twelve Apostles.

Roman Catholic That part of the Church owing loyalty to the Bishop of Rome, as distinct from Orthodox and Protestant Churches. The word 'catholic' means universal or worldwide.

denomination A group of churches within Christianity which follow a set of beliefs and practices, for example the Church of England.

ecumenical A movement that brings different churches together.

liturgical Service of worship according to a prescribed ritual such as Evensong or Eucharist.

orthodox Correct or true beliefs; also refers to denominations.

Pope The Bishop of Rome, head of the Roman Catholic Church.

Protestant A church that has 'protested' against the Roman Catholic Church and created its own denomination.

purgatory In some traditions, a condition or state in which good souls receive spiritual cleansing after death, in preparation for Heaven.

sacrament An outward visible sign of an inward spiritual grace, as in e.g. baptism or the Eucharist.

seven sacraments Roman Catholics believe there are seven sacraments which show God at work in people's lives and make people feel close to God. The seven sacraments are baptism, confirmation, marriage, ordination, anointing of the sick, eucharist and reconciliation.

seven sacred mysteries The Orthodox Church believes there are seven sacred mysteries which show God at work in people's lives and make people feel close to God. The seven sacred mysteries are baptism, chrismation, marriage, ordination, anointing of the sick, the Divine Liturgy and reconciliation.

FOR INTEREST Using either the Yellow Pages for your area, or the Thomson local directory, under places of worship look at the number of different Christian churches. Keep a tally chart for Roman Catholic, Orthodox, Church of England, Baptist, Methodist, United Reformed. Make a note of any others. Do you have other religious buildings listed – mosques, gurdwaras, mandirs, synagogues, temples? Analyse your results. What have you learnt about the religions and Christian churches in your local area?

How did Christian denominations come into being?

The next two pages will help you to:

- explain how different Christian **denominations** came into being
- identify what beliefs, practices, sources of authority and styles of worship Christian denominations have in common
- reflect on whether you think the reasons for splitting into denominations were sufficient.

An Orthodox priest.

A Roman Catholic priest.

Pentecost

Pentecost is when the Holy Spirit descended in tongues of fire to the disciples, shortly after the Ascension (see Topic 2.3). Pentecost marks the beginning of the Christian church. Two of the most important people in spreading Christianity after Pentecost were Simon Peter and Paul (who was originally called Saul of Tarsus). The book of Acts in the Bible records how it happened. For several hundred years after Jesus it was not easy to be a Christian. Christians faced persecution, and even death, because they worshipped God. The Roman Empire expected everyone to make the Roman emperor the most important person.

Things changed when Constantine became emperor and became a Christian in 325 CE – Christianity was officially allowed in the Roman Empire.

AO1 skills **ACTIVITIES**

Read Acts 9:1–19 to discover how Saul became a Christian. How would you explain what happened to him?

 **RESEARCH NOTE**

One of the infamous Roman emperors who persecuted Christians was the Emperor Nero. Research his life and his behaviour.

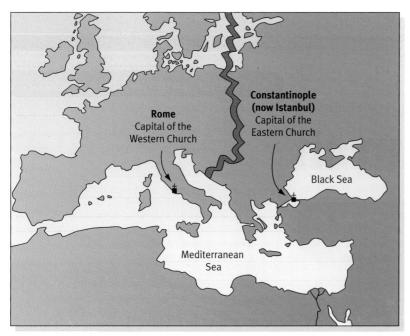

The following timeline charts the development of the Christian Church from 1054.

1054 CE: The Great Schism. The Pope and the Patriarch of Constantinople disagree. Why? The Eastern and Western Churches disagreed over a line in the Nicene Creed. Does the Holy Spirit come from God the Father or from both God the Father and Jesus?

- In the Orthodox Church the words in the Creed are: We believe in the Holy Spirit, the Lord, the giver of life, who proceeds from the Father. The Roman Catholic Church has: We believe in the Holy Spirit, the Lord, the giver of life, who proceeds from the Father and the Son.

1517 CE: The Reformation. In Germany a monk, Martin Luther, published his '95 theses' or complaints about the Roman Catholic Church. He argued that the Roman Catholic Church had forgotten Jesus' message and was corrupt and that it needed to reform. He argued that:

- Christians can pray to God direct – they don't need a priest

- The Bible should be read by any Christian, not just the priests, and is the most important source of authority, not the Pope

- Christianity is about having faith in God not about buying salvation. The church was making a lot of money charging people to have their time in purgatory shortened.

Christians who protested against the Roman Catholic Church created their own Churches, called Protestant Churches, e.g. Lutheran, Reformed Church, Anabaptists, Church of England.

17th and 18th century CE: Some Christians protested against the Church of England as it was not reformed enough.

19th century CE: They were called Nonconformist because they did not conform to the Church of England.

20th century CE: These denominations evolved from the Church of England. Some examples are Methodist, Baptist, the Salvation Army, Quakers and Pentecostal Churches.

ACTIVITIES

Answer the following questions to see how much you know about this topic before you begin.

1 What does denomination mean?
2 Name two different Christian denominations.
3 Name two of the twelve disciples.
4 What country did Christianity originate in?
5 What does 'catholic' mean?
6 What does 'orthodox' mean?
7 A Protestant church means one which protested against which other church?

ACTIVITIES

Is there anything you believe in strongly enough to die for it? Jesus told his followers to turn the other cheek and to love their neighbour as they loved themselves. So why did the Roman emperors see Christians as such a threat?

ACTIVITIES

Discuss with a partner whether you think the reasons for splitting into denominations were sufficient. When were the key moments? Do you think something could have been done to prevent the split? Share your views with the rest of the class.

The Roman Catholic Church

The next two pages will help you to:

- explore the beliefs, organisation and sources of authority of the Roman Catholic Church
- explore the worship and practices of the Roman Catholic Church
- evaluate Roman Catholic attitudes towards unmarried priests and moral issues.

Interior of Brompton Oratory, London, a Roman Catholic church.

Organisation and sources of authority

The Roman Catholic Church is organised in a worldwide hierarchy under the **Pope** and the Roman Curia. Archbishops and bishops administer individual dioceses as successors of the Twelve Apostles. The archbishops and bishops are responsible for the appointment and supervision of parish priests, and the oversight of all Church affairs within their diocese.

The Pope traces his role back to Jesus because of his words to Simon Peter in Matthew 16:18, 19. Peter became the first Bishop of Rome and his authority has been passed on in an unbroken chain to each Pope through the laying on of hands. This is called the **Apostolic succession**.

 **ACTIVITIES**

Who is the current Pope? How is a Pope elected? What is so unique about the Vatican City?

> **Matthew 16:18, 19**
>
> *And I tell you that you are Peter, and on this rock I will build my church... I will give you the keys of the kingdom of heaven; whatever you bind on earth will be bound in heaven, and whatever you loose on earth will be loosed in heaven.*

The Pope is God's living representative on Earth and he has the authority to speak on behalf of God on important matters, especially when the Bible does not give an answer; for example, what contraception to use. His authority is infallible. The Pope appoints all the cardinals and bishops.

England and Wales share a cardinal and both Scotland and Ireland have one. Bishops are in charge of a smaller area in a country, known as a diocese. The parish priest is in the local church and leads services and looks after the laity (congregation). There are no women priests because Jesus was male and as a priest represents Jesus he has to be male.

Roman Catholic beliefs, worship and practices

- Roman Catholics accept the beliefs found in the Apostles' Creed and also believe in **purgatory**.

- Roman Catholics use the Bible for help on how to live as a Christian but rely on the **Pope** for further guidance. There are also extra books in the Roman Catholic Bible, in the Old Testament, known to Protestants as the Apocrypha.

- Roman Catholics practise Jesus' example of loving and caring for other people.

- Roman Catholics believe there are **seven sacraments** which show God at work in people's lives and make people feel close to God. The seven sacraments are baptism, confirmation, marriage, ordination, anointing of the sick, the eucharist and reconciliation.

- Roman Catholics believe undertaking pilgrimage is important.

- Mary, Jesus' mother, is given much respect. Catholics believe in the Immaculate Conception of Mary (she was born without sin) and in her bodily Assumption to Heaven at the end of her life. Many churches have statues of Mary and her help is often sought during prayer. A famous prayer is the Hail Mary.

- Saints are important as role models for Christians to copy and because they give an insight into God's character.

- Church services follow a **liturgical** (set order) style. The aim of the service is to bring people closer to God and strengthen their relationship with him. Reconciliation or confession of sin is encouraged.

- Transubstantiation. During the eucharist the bread and wine become Jesus' body and blood. This is why the focal point in a church is the altar.

- Churches are purpose-built buildings full of symbols and features to help a Christian think about God and feel closer to him.

- If people want to dedicate their life to God becoming a monk or nun is encouraged.

- The Roman Catholic Church takes a very strong view on the value of human life, and is against abortion, euthanasia and artificial methods of contraception.

ACTIVITIES

Consider the following controversial topics in pairs and then discuss with the rest of the class.

- What are the advantages and disadvantages of having an unmarried priest?
- 'Pregnant at 13, mum at 14, GCSEs at 15.' What would a Roman Catholic think about this situation?

Until the Second Vatican Council in the 1960s most Roman Catholic church services were held in Latin. Since then services have usually been held in the language of the country. What do you think might be the advantages and disadvantages of holding services in Latin?

The Orthodox Church

The Orthodox Church

While the Roman Catholic Church developed in Western Europe and was then carried around the world by European explorers and travellers, the Orthodox Church developed in eastern Europe, the Mediterranean and North Africa. Around 200 million Christians belong to the Orthodox Church around the world but in Britain most Orthodox Christians are people who have migrated there and brought their **denomination** with them.

Organisation and sources of authority

The Orthodox Church is organised like learning communities in a school. The church in Greece is called the Greek Orthodox Church, the Church in Russia is called the Russian Orthodox Church.

In charge of the Church in each country is a patriarch. The patriarch is a senior bishop. The other bishops help him organise the Church. Bishops see their role as being the successors of the Apostles.

Bishops appoint priests to look after local churches but have to have the agreement of the congregation before the priest can start work.

Although each country's part of the Orthodox Church is independent, the Patriarch of Constantinople is given the added role of being the spiritual leader and spokesman for all Orthodox Christians. This prevents confusion arising and contradictory statements being given.

The Patriarch does not have the same kind of authority that the **Pope** has in the Roman Catholic Church. He is not believed to be infallible. The patriarchs and bishops believe they are guardians of Church tradition and history, and when asked for advice on an issue they will look at what the Bible says and at what the Church has said previously and apply that to the issue, for example abortion.

Only men can be priests, bishops and patriarchs because they are the successors of Jesus and his apostles. Married men may become priests, but bishops and patriarchs must remain unmarried.

Orthodox beliefs, worship and practices

- The Orthodox Church accepts the beliefs found in the Apostles' Creed, although they have a different statement about the Holy Spirit in the Nicene Creed.
- The Orthodox Church uses the Bible for help on how to live as a Christian but also refers to Church tradition.

The next two pages will help you to:

- explore the beliefs, organisation, sources of authority, worship and practices of the **Orthodox** Church
- compare and contrast features in the **Roman Catholic** and Orthodox Churches.

 **ACTIVITIES**

Why do you think the role of spiritual leader always goes to the Patriarch of Constantinople? Think back to the history of Christianity and the timeline page.

The Didache 2.2
Do not murder a child by abortion.

- The Orthodox Church practises Jesus' example of loving and caring for other people.
- The Orthodox Church believes there are **seven sacred mysteries** that show God at work in people's lives and make people feel close to God. The seven sacred mysteries are baptism, chrismation, marriage, ordination, anointing of the sick, the Divine Liturgy and reconciliation.
- Mary, the mother of Jesus, and the saints are given much respect. Every day in the Orthodox calendar is a saint's day.
- Church services follow a **liturgical** (set order) style. The aim of the service is to bring people closer to God, strengthen their relationship with God and in some way give people a sense of what Heaven will be like.
- The most important service is the Divine Liturgy (Eucharist). The bread and wine become Jesus' body and blood in some sacred, mysterious way. This re-enacts Jesus' incarnation, death and resurrection and all that they mean for Christians.
- Churches are purpose-built buildings full of symbols and features to help a Christian think about God and feel closer to him.
- If people want to dedicate their life to God, becoming a monk is encouraged.
- Fasting, self-discipline and prayer must be practised as they bring people closer to God and make them into better Christians. The 'Jesus prayer' is used for meditation. Confession of sins is also important.

ACTIVITIES

What are the seven deadly sins? How would applying Orthodox practices of fasting, self-discipline and meditation help lessen the temptation to commit these sins? Most Orthodox Christians wear a visible sign of being a Christian, usually a cross on a chain necklace. Is this a good idea?

REMEMBER THIS

Chrismation A sacrament in which a baptised person is anointed with chrism (consecrated oil).

GradeStudio

AO1

QUESTION

Explain why Roman Catholics and Orthodox Christians worship in different ways. **[6 marks]**

This is an AO1 question, meaning it is testing your knowledge and understanding. As we've seen in previous Grade Studios, examiners will use three levels to measure how successfully you demonstrate these skills.

Note that this is the only section of the specification where you have to be able to respond with knowledge and understanding of more than one denomination.

This question is asking for the reasons for differences in worship. One way to approach this is to refer to the history of the two denominations that leads to the differences in authority and practice. You could build a response in this way:

Level 1

Start with a simple statement about how the differences in ways of worship can be explained because the two denominations have communicated little with each other since they split many centuries ago and their worship and practices have developed along different lines.

Level 2

Develop this further by referring to differences in authority which have resulted from the split. For example, Roman Catholics and Orthodox Christians look to different people to guide them. Roman Catholics are guided by the Pope but Orthodox Christians do not accept his authority. When the Pope says how Christians should worship this does not affect Orthodox Christians which leads to differences.

Level 3

Finally, expand the issue of authority with reference, for example, to the fact that most Roman Catholic worship is conducted in the local language, which contrasts with the use of ancient liturgy by Orthodox Christians.

Or suggest other reasons such as: difference in calendars leading to celebrating the same events at different times and in different ways or to the use of icons by Orthodox Christians to help them concentrate in worship whilst Roman Catholics prefer other artefacts.

Protestant Churches 1

The Protestant Church

By doing the denomination activity you should have found that the Church of England has the most churches. There are lots of other **Protestant** churches but fewer **Roman Catholic** or **Orthodox** churches. The previous chapter explained why there were few Orthodox churches in Britain, but why are there few Roman Catholic churches and so many Protestant ones?

The answer lies in history and begins with Henry VIII. Henry VIII was King of England between 1509 and 1547. The only Church that anyone could attend was the Roman Catholic Church but some people in England had heard of Martin Luther's protest in Germany, liked his ideas and wanted to see reform in England. Henry VIII was not interested in reforming the Roman Catholic Church until he wanted a divorce from his wife, Catherine of Aragon, so he could marry his mistress, Anne Boleyn. The Pope refused to allow a divorce.

Henry's solution? Reject the authority of the Pope and the Roman Catholic Church. Henry made himself 'the Supreme Head' and 'Defender of the Faith' of the Church in England. This became the official religion in England. Now as head of the Church he could grant himself a divorce.

When Henry VIII died, his son, Edward VI, was too young and too sick to rule so a council of nobles ruled England. These nobles were mostly Protestants and they brought Protestant teachings to the Church of England. When Edward died in 1553, the English people wanted Henry's daughter Mary to rule England. Mary was Catholic so when she became queen, she accepted the Pope as the head of the Church in England and said all English people had to return to the Catholic Church. Protestants who refused were harshly punished.

When Elizabeth I was made Queen in 1558, she inherited a nation that was caught between Protestantism and Catholicism – or a middle way.

Church of England

So, have you worked out why there are so few Catholic churches but so many Church of England ones?

In the 21st century, the Church of England is still the state religion in Britain. The monarch has to belong to this denomination and most royal christenings, weddings and funerals take place in the Church of England. Bishops of the Church of England sit in the House of Lords in Parliament.

The next two pages will help you to:

- explore the beliefs, organisation, sources of authority, worship and practices in the Church of England
- explain why the Church of England is called 'the middle way'
- consider the Church of England as the state religion of Britain.

AO1 skills **ACTIVITIES**

Remember the counting of different **denominations** in the phone directories that you did at the beginning of this Topic? What can you remember? List as many different denominations as you can. Which denomination had the most churches?

Henry VIII who rejected the authority of the Pope and made himself the supreme head of the Church in England.

As the Church of England is the state religion, it had to be possible for everyone in the country to have access to a Church of England church as they had to attend services every Sunday. Even today, everyone has the right to ask for a christening, their wedding or a funeral service at their local church, even if they do not regularly attend.

With the development of the British Empire, the Church of England became known as the **Anglican Church** and can be found in Africa, India, Asia, America, Canada, etc.

Organisation and sources of authority

Each country's Anglican Church governs itself but the Archbishop of Canterbury is given the role as the spiritual leader and spokesman for all Anglican churches in the world. Every ten years there is a big assembly called the Lambeth Conference (the last one was in 2008) where all the Anglican bishops from around the world can meet to discuss issues affecting the Anglican Church and show their unity.

Bishops and archbishops see their role as the successors of Jesus' disciples. As a Protestant church, its source of authority is the Bible but sometimes answers are not obvious and reason and conscience should be used. Church tradition can also be consulted.

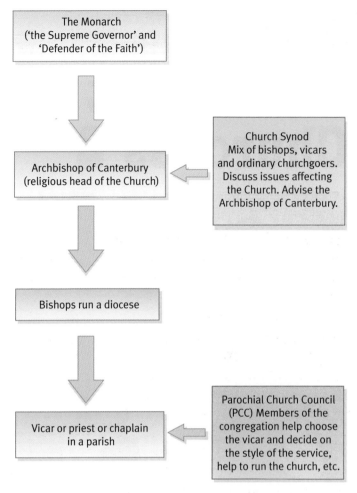

Church of England beliefs, worship and practices

- The Church of England accepts the beliefs found in the Apostles' Creed.

- The Church of England uses the Bible for help on how to live as a Christian but also uses reason, conscience and tradition if necessary.

- The Church of England practises Jesus' example of loving and caring for other people.

- The Church of England believes there are two **sacraments** – baptism and the eucharist. These are the only sacraments specifically mentioned in the Bible but some Anglicans believe in all seven sacraments, agreeing with the teachings of the Roman Catholic Church.

- There is a wide variety of views within the Anglican Church about what a church service should be like, how the building should be decorated and what it should teach on moral issues.

- Some churches are more like Roman Catholic churches. Others are more like Nonconformist churches.

- At the Eucharist the bread and wine are usually seen as being the body and blood of Jesus but not in quite the same way as the Roman Catholic Church teaches.

ACTIVITIES

The Church of England is sometimes called 'the middle way'. What do you think this means? Prince Charles when he becomes king wants to change his title to 'Defender of Faiths' as Britain is a multi-faith society. Do you think he is right to do this?

Protestant Churches 2

The next two pages will help you to:

- explore the beliefs, organisation, sources of authority, worship and practices in another **Protestant** Church
- compare and contrast **denominations**
- evaluate whether the denominations should resolve their differences and unite as one Church
- consider if having many denominations is a good or a bad thing for Christians.

Worshippers in a Pentecostal Church.

ACTIVITIES

Invite your music teacher to your lesson to play you pieces of music found in Roman Catholic, Orthodox and Protestant Churches. What feelings does each piece of music arouse in you? Can you guess which music is more likely to be found in which denomination?

Non-conforming churches

Within a hundred years of Henry VIII creating the Church in England, protests began against it.

These Churches did not conform to the state religion so they were called **non-conforming** Churches or **Free** Churches. Some of the most well known are Methodists, Baptists, the Religious Society of Friends (Quakers), the Salvation Army and the Pentecostal Churches.

Some of these have non-liturgical (no set order) services – the most important part can be a sermon, singing or silence depending on the denomination. Services can take place anywhere. Some have two **sacraments**, some have none. The important thing is to be inspired and encouraged to live a Christian way of life during the rest of the week. The Bible and a Christian's own conscience are consulted when a decision needs to be made.

As Free Churches they do not have a leadership hierarchy and have only loose links to other similar Churches but probably have an association they belong to which will speak on their behalf if required, for example the Baptist Union or the Evangelical Alliance.

AO1 skills **ACTIVITIES**

Choose from one of the non-conforming Churches (Baptists, Quakers, the Salvation Army and Pentecostal) and create a fact file about it. Investigate how it organises itself, what is the service like and what makes this denomination different from other denominations. Then, write a one-minute speech to persuade people to join this denomination and perform to the class.

Compare and contrast denominations

AO2 skills **ACTIVITIES**

The previous sections have included a lot of information that needs to be processed into an easy-to-remember way. Copy the table below and make a list of the similarities and differences between these denominations. Discuss these with the rest of the class and consider whether the different denominations are so similar that they should resolve their differences and unite.

	Roman Catholic	Orthodox	Protestant – Church of England	Protestant – Nonconformist
Beliefs				
Organisation				
Sources of authority				
Worship and practices				

Churches working together: Ecumenism 1

Ecumenism

Ecumenical is derived from the Greek word *oikoumene* which means '*of the inhabited earth*'. The ecumenical movement aims to bring all churches together in unity, remembering that they are all followers of Jesus and worship the same God. Supporters of ecumenism argue Jesus would never have wanted Christians to argue amongst themselves and divide into different denominations.

> **1 Corinthians 12:27**
>
> *Now you are the body of Christ, and each one of you is a part of it.*

> **Matthew 22:39**
>
> *Love your neighbour as yourself.*

Important developments in the history of ecumenicism include:

- 1910 Edinburgh, Scotland. Churches discuss how they can work together in foreign countries. Can missionaries working for different Churches stop competing for converts and share resources and buildings?

- 1927 Lausanne, Switzerland. A multi-denominational conference to discuss differences between different denominations.

- 1948 The World Council of Churches was formed after World War II (1939–1945). Every member must accept the Christian belief that Jesus Christ is God and Saviour of the world and that Christians are 'All one in Christ'.

The aim of the World Council of Churches was to encourage world peace and unity following World War II. If Christians from around the world and from different denominations can talk together and discuss their differences, why can't countries? If Christians can work together to encourage peace and justice by helping others in need it would set a good example for everyone else to follow. The Council works through many aid agencies, for example Christian Aid in Britain.

The next two pages will help you to:

- explore the organisation and practices of ecumenism
- explore the work of the World Council of Churches
- consider whether differences between **denominations** can or should be resolved.

A01 skills ACTIVITIES

Scenario: A member of your class is trying to organise a class trip to the cinema with a meal but is having trouble deciding where to eat and what film to watch so that everyone will come. In groups decide where to eat and which film to see. Was it easy to reach agreement? Did you have to compromise? Is everyone going to attend? Why or why not? Would your differences stop you from being friends? What are the possible solutions?

Initially, 148 **Protestant** Churches joined. Since then, more Protestant denominations have joined. The **Orthodox** Church joined in 1961 and, although the **Roman Catholic** Church has not officially joined, it sends official observers. The Council aims to meet every eight years.

An example of an ecumenical organisation

The logo of the World Council of Churches

Some topics that have been discussed at the World Council of Churches include:

- Theological differences between different churches: for example what actually happens at the Eucharist? Is it a reminder of Jesus' death and sacrifice or do the bread and wine transubstantiate into Jesus' body and blood?
- What makes a person a Christian? Is it baptism? Living a Christian life? Personal repentance and asking for your sins to be forgiven? A combination of these?
- War – is it right for Christians to fight?
- Racism.
- Homosexuality.
- Poverty.

ACTIVITIES

Can the differences between denominations be resolved? Working in small groups choose one of the topics (left) and research what three different denominations think about it. Compare them – where do they agree? Where do they disagree? Can you suggest a way they might compromise in their views? Do you think it is possible to reach an agreement?

Churches working together:
Ecumenism 2

How does ecumenism work in Britain?

The next two pages will help you to:

- explore how ecumenism works in modern Britain
- evaluate some examples of denominations working together despite their differences.

Once denominations start talking to each other, some of them find they have so many things in common and, where they have differences, they can compromise so they decide to unite. So far this has been among smaller denominations; for example, the Presbyterian and Congregational denominations became the United Reformed Church in 1972. There have also been discussions about the Methodist Church reuniting with the Church of England (it began because of disagreements with the Church of England back in the 18th century).

However, strong feelings are sometimes aroused when Church of England and **Roman Catholic** Church leaders appear to agree.

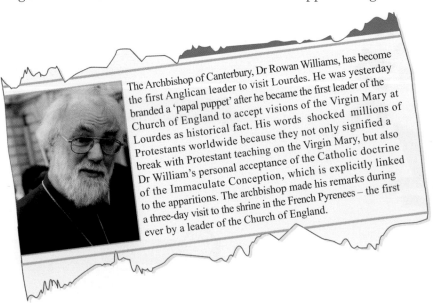

The Archbishop of Canterbury, Dr Rowan Williams, has become the first Anglican leader to visit Lourdes. He was yesterday branded a 'papal puppet' after he became the first leader of the Church of England to accept visions of the Virgin Mary at Lourdes as historical fact. His words shocked millions of Protestants worldwide because they not only signified a break with Protestant teaching on the Virgin Mary, but also Dr William's personal acceptance of the Catholic doctrine of the Immaculate Conception, which is explicitly linked to the apparitions. The archbishop made his remarks during a three-day visit to the shrine in the French Pyrenees – the first ever by a leader of the Church of England.

Following his vist to Lourdes, Rowan Williams was severely criticised. The Reverend Jeremy Brooks said: 'All true **Protestant**s will be appalled that the Archbishop of Canterbury has visited Lourdes, and preached there. Lourdes represents everything about Roman Catholicism that the Protestant Reformation rejected, including apparitions, mariolatry and the veneration of saints.'

Most ecumenical work takes place between individual Christians who are either friends who attend different churches, or Christians who live locally and are concerned by something happening in their local area.

AO1 skills ACTIVITIES

Local churches would like a logo to use that symbolises the work that they are trying to do in bringing church communities together. Design a logo that demonstrates their commitment to **ecumenical** practice but also their individuality.

Some ecumenical groups in Britain

- 'Churches Together in Britain and Ireland' acts as a central point for any churches wishing to work together – the offices, staff and website share examples of good practice and offer advice.
- 'Churches for All' helps churches become disability friendly. How can churches best adapt buildings for wheelchairs, blind or partially sighted people and the hard of hearing? How can churches involve physically and mentally disabled people in youth groups or musical groups?
- 'More Than Gold' encourages churches to work together to serve sport and the community. Its aim is to involve Christians in London's 2012 Olympics. It wants churches to offer hospitality for athletes' families, provide chaplains to the Olympic village, and offer care and refreshments for spectators.

Shared churches and worship

Different churches are sharing buildings and holding joint services either because the number of people attending church has fallen or because new housing estates are being built and Christians want to have a presence there. This means sharing a building.

Two churches that have joined together in one building are St Chad's Church of England Church and St John's Hill Methodist Church in Shrewsbury. They share a building, have common services and activities, for example Lenten lunches but have also kept distinct services and groups.

 **RESEARCH NOTE**

Contact your local churches and find out how they work together.

 **ACTIVITIES**

You are on an ecumenical working party that has the task of drawing up plans for an ecumenical church for a new housing estate. The following denominations have agreed to share a building and a youth worker: Church of England, Pentecostal and Roman Catholic. Consider the ways that these denominations can work together and the practicalities. Your plans must give detailed reasons for your choices and explain where it was difficult to reach consensus.

 GradeStudio

AO1

QUESTION

Explain why and how Christians from different denominations are working together today. **[6 marks]**

This is an AO1 question, asking for understanding and knowledge in that order. So the first task is to explain why Christians want to work together today and then to go on to give examples of how this is put into practice. Remember there are three levels for AO1.

Level 1

Christians want to work together today because they see that although there are differences, they all belong to the same faith, worship the same God and value Jesus in the same way. They realise the differences should not prevent them working together on things that they all believe to be important, like world poverty.

Level 2

Offer another *reason why* Christians want to work together, such as their need to put differences aside so they can unite in the face of secularism. Now go on to give examples of *how* Christians work together, such as in ecumenical communities like Iona or Corrymeela or through combined charitable activities. (Be concise when describing these as this question is only worth 6 marks.)

Level 3

Finally sum up suggesting, for example, that the differences show the richness of the Christian faith and that they need not come in the way of Christians getting on with each other in their practical activities.

Ecumenical communities:
Taizé, Iona and Corrymeela

The next two pages will help you to:

- explore the practices of the Taizé, Iona and Corrymeela communities
- explain why these communities are important to some Christians
- evaluate the advantages and disadvantages of visiting **ecumenical** communities.

Taizé

In 1940 Roger Schutz founded a religious community of monks at Taizé in France that sheltered Jewish refugees escaping Nazi Germany until 1942. When the Nazis occupied France, Roger had to leave but returned at the end of the war, initially caring for German prisoners of war, practising the Christian belief of forgiveness and reconciliation.

Taizé is a place of pilgrimage particularly for young people from all over the world and, as an ecumenical community, works to break down barriers between Christian **denominations**. The monks also are from different churches and different countries.

Young people camp in the fields, join in daily worship and help with practical work in the kitchens and on the farms. Worship includes simple songs in Latin, French, German and English. Music is central to the witness and life of Taizé. There is time for meditation and reflection allowing young people to develop self-awareness of what is in their heart and to listen to God. Times of group discussion encourage listening skills and a chance to discuss the challenges of being a young Christian. Living a simpler monastic life without television and luxuries helps people find a meaning to life and to decide what is really important.

Iona

The island of Iona is situated off the coast of Scotland and has a long history as a religious centre and place of pilgrimage. In 563 St Columba came to Iona with a group of monks hoping to convert local people to Christianity. The monastery was rebuilt in the 1930s by the Reverend George MacLeod and a group of unemployed people from Glasgow. Having experienced the benefits of living in a community, Reverend MacLeod hoped they would return home and encourage a community spirit and way of life in their city and neighbourhood.

Today Iona is a place where ministers and ordinary Christians come to spend a week living simply, spending time in prayer and reading the Bible. They can also reflect on how they spend their time and money and meet together to share their experiences of living as a Christian.

It is also an opportunity to discuss some of the problem areas and issues facing the world and work out how a Christian should respond to these problems. Recent issues have included global poverty and injustice, the environment and immigration.

RESEARCH NOTE

Taizé is a place visited primarily by young people and some have recorded their experiences on YouTube and on the Taizé website. View some of their video entries and record your impressions of Taizé and reflect on why it is so popular with young people.

MUST THINK ABOUT!

If there was an issue in the world today that the Iona community ought to be considering, what would it be and why?

AO1 skills ACTIVITIES

How would your neighbourhood or town change if people practised a community spirit?

St Mary's Abbey, Iona.

Corrymeela

" *If Christianity has nothing to say about reconciliation, then it has nothing to say.* **"**

These are the words of the founder of Corrymeela, Reverend Dr R.R. Davey. Corrymeela was established to provide an opportunity for reconciliation and developing understanding amongst people in Northern Ireland. When it was set up it was unique in Ireland.

Stephen (a **Protestant**) has been to stay at Corrymeela several times and had this to say about his experience.

" *Although Northern Ireland is peaceful now, before the Good Friday agreement in 1998 there was always the risk of a terrorist shooting or bomb by the IRA (who wanted a United Ireland) or by the UDA/UDF (who wanted Northern Ireland to stay part of the UK). Protestants and Catholics did not mix – we went to separate schools, had no friends who were Catholic, hardly anyone married a Catholic and we lived in different parts of Belfast.*

The first time I went [to Corrymeela] my school took us. We met pupils from Catholic schools and realised we weren't that different! I've been back several times now because it is still great to have time in a beautiful place to talk to people you wouldn't otherwise meet. Last time I went it was for a weekend on Third World Development and I met people from other countries. It opens your horizons. **"**

AO2 skills ACTIVITIES

Make a list of all the advantages of visiting an ecumenical community. What are the disadvantages of visiting an ecumenical community instead of your local church?

Challenges facing the Christian Church

Who should be a priest or a minister?

Should women be allowed to become vicars and priests? If so, should they also be allowed to become bishops?

The **Roman Catholic** and **Orthodox** Churches say no. Many **Protestant** Churches say yes. The Church of England ordained its first women vicars in 1994 and now has to decide if they should be allowed to become bishops.

> **Galatians 3: 28**
>
> *There is neither Jew nor Greek, slave nor free, male nor female, for you are all one in Christ Jesus.*

> **1 Corinthians 14:34a, 35b**
>
> *Women should remain silent in the churches. They are not allowed to speak... for it is disgraceful for a woman to speak in the church.*

Should homosexual men be vicars or priests? This became a high profile issue in 2003 when the Reverend Gene Robinson, an openly gay vicar, was appointed Bishop of New Hampshire in America and Canon Jeffrey John, a celibate homosexual, was appointed Bishop of Reading in Britain. Canon Jeffrey John did not take up his new job due to the resulting controversy.

Christian denominations have different views. Quakers are most accepting but many other churches say it is wrong. The Catholic Church says if you have homosexual tendencies but are celibate you are permitted to become a priest.

> **Romans 1:27**
>
> *In the same way the men also abandoned natural relations with women and were inflamed with lust for one another. Men committed indecent acts with other men, and received in themselves the due penalty for their perversion.*

One of the underlying reasons for differences between Christians is because of how they interpret the Bible – is it the Word of God and to be read literally or is it advice which needs to be reinterpreted to fit life in the 21st century? Who should do the reinterpreting – the **Pope** or an individual's conscience?

 MUST THINK ABOUT!

What do you think about women vicars and homosexual priests? Is the Bible wrong if it contradicts itself as it appears to over women vicars? Is there a significant difference between being a practising homosexual and being a celibate one? Is the Bible saying any homosexual tendencies are wrong?

 **ACTIVITIES**

Choose one of the issues on this spread and investigate further. You need to know five facts about the issue and two different Christian responses to it. You could swap your work for someone else's on a different issue. If you had to make a prediction about what issues the church would be facing in 2050 what would you say? Explain your ideas. Do you think Christianity will still exist in 2050?

Do the churches in Africa, Asia and South America have anything in common with churches in Europe and North America?

Archbishop Desmond Tutu has accused the **Anglican Church** of allowing its 'obsession' with homosexuality to come before real action on world poverty. 'God is weeping' to see such a focus on sexuality and the Church is 'quite rightly' seen by many as irrelevant on the issue of poverty (BBC website 2008).

Outside of Europe and North America all denominations are growing, especially Pentecostal and evangelical denominations. The debate over homosexuality does not exist unless it is to express anger that Churches in Europe and North America are not dealing with the most important issues such as:

AIDS: some 25 million people worldwide live with HIV and up to 12 million children are orphaned because of AIDS. The Roman Catholic Church does not allow the use of artificial methods of contraception and yet condoms are recommended as a way of preventing the spread of HIV/AIDS.

Poverty and social injustice: some 30,000 people die every day in the world from poverty and social injustice. In South America liberation theology has developed, particularly amongst Roman Catholics, as a way of encouraging people to fight injustice, corruption and poverty. However, the Pope has condemned it.

Environment: what is the Christian Church saying and doing about environmental concerns? Most environmental damage is done by Europe and North America. Poorer countries are most affected by the consequences.

Multi-faith: the world is increasingly multi-faith as people travel more and live in different countries. Should Christians evangelise? Is Christianity the true religion and only way of finding God (an exclusive attitude) or are other religions also true (an inclusive attitude)?

 GradeStudio

AO2

QUESTION
Differences between Christians show the faith to be weak.
[12 marks]

This is an AO2 question, so examiners will be looking to see how well you can present differing points of view. They will want to see evidence and reasoned argument in support of them, as well as a conclusion with your own point of view. Remember, they will use four levels to assess your response. Identify the issue in the question – which is that differences and divisions in Christianity make it weak. A response could be built up in this way.

Level 1
Start with a simple statement of a point of view, for example: all organisations that have disagreement or are divided eventually fail. Christianity is no different and unless Christians agree on everything the faith will be weak and will eventually disappear.

Level 2
Develop the statement with some support such as: over the centuries Christians have spent time fighting each other when they could have been spreading the faith or putting their faith into practice. As a result the faith seems irrelevant to much of the modern world.

Level 3
Now give a different point of view and support it with evidence and argument, for example people differ and there is nothing wrong with the differences as this enables different people to enjoy and belong to the faith in their own way. In fact, the differences make the faith more attractive and stronger. Give your own view.

Level 4
Finally, weigh up points of view against each other and explain your own personal response and support it with evidence and argument. Your view might be that differences are good, provided everybody can accept each other. Or you might say that unfortunately the history of Christianity shows that the differences were too great to allow Christians to work with each other. This led to weakness and, in the modern world, to a lack of interest in the faith.

Welcome to the Grade Studio

In this Grade Studio we are going to look at how to build a really good response to an AO2 question. You will use your knowledge and understanding of the beliefs, organisation and practices of different Christian groups to inform the discussions.

Graded examples for this topic

AO2

Although they are called questions, AO2 questions are really statements for discussion such as:

Question

Christians believe in the same God, so they should all worship in the same way.　　　**[12 marks]**

Here is a framework that could be used to build a response to the statement.

Step 1: Understand the issue in the question.

The question/statement is saying a) that all Christians believe in the same God and b) this means that Christians should all practise their religion in the same way. The debate is not about a). It is about whether it is appropriate for Christians to worship in different ways.

Step 2: Identify different attitudes to the issue.
- Attitudes do not need to be opposites.
- You could do this by drawing a spider diagram where you write down anything that could be connected with this issue.

The spider diagram could include:
- believing in God is a key point of the Christian faith and it is something all Christians share
- worship is bound to differ because of historical differences and splits between Christian groups
- people have different personalities and like to express their feelings in different ways and need different forms of worship
- Christians may all believe in the same God, but there is a lot more to Christianity than that; it depends on different attitudes to Jesus, religious authority, interpretations of the Bible
- provided all Christians accept that however they or other Christians worship, it is just a way of worshipping God in spirit and truth which is as good as any other then it does not matter
- decide on your own view.

Step 3: Check you can support the ideas with evidence – knowledge to underpin each view you wish to use.
Note this information briefly on the spider diagram.

A good response does not need to cover every aspect of the debate, provided the views chosen are well developed and supported. You might not use everything on the spider diagram.

Step 4: Start writing your response.
Begin by telling the examiner briefly what the issue is and then explain the views you have decided to use.

Back each view up with evidence and make a comment about how this affects the discussion.

Step 5: Conclude with your view.

The best responses will draw all the ideas together and sum up the debate with their own comment supported by evidence.

Draw up your own table, research and write a response using this framework. Then compare what you have done with this sample response.

Introduction
The issue here is: should Christians have different ways of worship when they all believe in the same God? This response will look at why there are differences in the ways Christians worship and decide if differences are appropriate considering they are all worshipping the same God.

Student's answer

There are differences for historical reasons. Right from the start of the faith, Christians have had different views. Circumcision and the gift of speaking in tongues caused debate amongst the first Christians. As the faith developed new disagreements arose as Christians tried to understand and explain their faith that led to differences in worship. For example differences arose between Protestants with their focus on the Bible and preaching in worship, and the Roman Catholics with their emphasis on the celebration of the Eucharist.

There are differences because people are different. The same sort of worship does not suit everybody. Some people like to express their feelings openly and their faith is so important that they want to sing, shout and even dance to express it. Others are more reserved and want a more formal kind of worship because they find expressing emotion more difficult. It does not make one form more valid than another. People are different and worship needs to be different to meet their needs.

It is true all Christians believe in God, but there are other key beliefs in Christianity. Not all Christians believe the same about them. Not all Christians use the same authority – some just follow the Bible which can be interpreted differently by people, whilst others also follow the guidance of the Pope.

People differ in the ways they do everything else, so why not in the way they worship?

My view is that if all Christians worshipped in the same way it would be very boring and would restrict personal expression and the faith would be unattractive to people. New developments in Christianity, for example with house churches, are leading to new forms of worship which are just as valid and more relevant to 21st-century Christians.

Conclusion
Jesus said people should worship God in spirit and in truth. Christians can't do that if the form of worship is out of touch with what they believe or is out of date, so although they all believe in the same God worship has to be different to be appropriate.

Examiner's comment

This is a **good** response because it shows a clear understanding of the question, offers several viewpoints and a personal view supported by evidence. The response is well organised and there is a clear reference to Christianity.

These specimen answers provide an outline of how you could construct your response. Space does not allow us to give a full response. The examiner will be looking for more detail in your actual exam responses.

Remember and Reflect

AO1 Describe, explain and analyse, using knowledge and understanding

Find the answer on:

1 What does the word denomination mean? Give three examples of Christian denominations.
PAGE 52

2 Name three things all denominations have in common.
PAGE 52

3 Name three things some denominations disagree on.
PAGE 52

4 What do the following terms mean?
a *Roman Catholic*   b *Orthodox*   c *Protestant*   d *Nonconformist*
PAGE 53, 63

5 What Christian festival celebrates the birth of the Church?
PAGE 54

6 What is the split between the Roman Catholic Church and the Orthodox Church called?
PAGE 55

7 When did Protestant Churches come into being?
PAGE 55

8 Explain how the Roman Catholic Church is organised.
PAGE 56, 57

9 What are the sources of authority a Roman Catholic will consult when making a decision?
PAGE 57

10 Explain why these sources have authority.
PAGE 56, 57

11 Explain how the Orthodox Church is organised.
PAGE 58

12 What is the biggest denomination in Britain? Explain briefly why this is so.
PAGE 60

13 What is this denomination called outside Britain?
PAGE 61

14 Name a Nonconformist Church. Give five ways it is different to the Roman Catholic, Orthodox and Church of England denominations.
PAGE 63

15 What does the word 'ecumenical' mean?
PAGE 64

16 Explain the aims of the World Council of Churches.
PAGE 64

17 Explain three ways different denominations and churches are working together in Britain.
PAGE 67

18 Name an ecumenical community and explain why it started and what its aims are.
PAGE 68, 69

19 Explain why some Christians find it helpful visiting an ecumenical community.
PAGE 68, 69

20 Outline two challenges facing the Christian Church in the 21st century. Why are they challenges?
PAGE 70, 71

21 Explain how the Church is responding to the two challenges you mentioned in the previous question.
PAGE 70, 71

AO2 Use evidence and reasoned argument to express and evaluate personal responses, informed insights, and differing viewpoints

Women ministers now play an important part in the life of the Church.

Answer the following, giving as much detail as possible. You should give at least three reasons to support your response and also show that you have taken into account different opinions.

1. Do you think Christianity has too many denominations?

2. Christians believe in the same God, so they should all worship in the same way. How far do you agree?

3. Christian denominations have more in common than they have differences. Do you agree?

4. Women vicars are the future – all churches should have them. True or false?

5. Is the increase in ecumenical work a good or bad thing for Christianity?

Topic 4: Places and forms of worship

The Big Picture

In this Topic you will **examine places and forms of Christian worship,** including:

- what places of worship might look like and what they show about what Christians believe
- key features of Christian places of worship, their meaning and purpose
- ways that Christians express their beliefs through different forms of worship.

You will also consider this Topic from the perspective of a range of Christian denominations.

What?

You will:

- develop your knowledge and understanding of the purpose and use of Christian places of worship
- explain how worship expresses Christian beliefs
- explore the links between belief and action in your own life.

How?

By:

- identifying and describing the key features of Christian places of worship
- connecting the use and purpose of places of worship with Christian beliefs
- comparing and contrasting the different forms of worship used by Christians.

Why?

Because:

- worship is an important feature of Christian belief and one which affects Christians' lives and those of their communities
- exploring the meanings behind the ways in which Christians worship will enable you to apply and extend your understanding of Christian beliefs
- understanding that our beliefs affect our actions helps you to consider the meaning of other people's actions as well as your own.

Look at the events listed below that you might attend. Can you work out what they have in common? Do you think that there are any which don't fit or are they all similar in some way? Try to explain your reasoning to your classmates.

- A Premiership football game.
- A birthday party with your family and friends.
- School assembly.
- A demonstration where you are one of the protestors.
- A friend's wedding.

A priest celebrating the Eucharist.

Places and forms of worship

KEY INFORMATION

- The word 'church' has a number of meanings. The most common use of the word church is to describe a building in which Christians worship.

- Not all denominations of Christianity call their place of worship a church but many do and therefore the word is often used to describe all Christian places of worship.

- Christians may worship in a church, or other place of worship, but can also worship at home.

- Not all church buildings were designed as places of worship. The importance of the building is not what it looks like but what happens inside.

- The majority of Christian denominations hold services for worship on Sundays.

- There is no one set way in which Christians worship in a church. This varies both between the denominations and within them too. Every Christian place of worship is unique.

- Some services are liturgical (this means that they follow a set pattern) but others are non-liturgical (they are less structured).

- One way in which many Christians worship is to take part in the sharing of bread and wine amongst the congregation. This service is a Eucharist but there are a number of names for this including Holy Communion and Mass. This reminds Christians of the Last Supper.

- Prayer is a common feature of worship both at home and in churches.

- The name of the leader of Christian worship in a place of worship varies. Common names include vicar, priest and minister.

- Not all church services are led. Some are less formal and members of the congregation may take a key role in the service.

KEY QUESTIONS

KNOWLEDGE AND UNDERSTANDING

How do Christians worship God?

In what way does worship help Christians express what they believe about God?

ANALYSIS AND EVALUATION

'Christians should go to church every Sunday to worship.' What do you think about this statement? How do you think Christians would respond to it?

annunciation The time when the Angel Gabriel visited Mary to announce to her that she would give birth to a baby.

church The word has three meanings: (i) The whole community of Christians, (ii) the building in which Christians worship and (iii) a particular denomination.

clergy Members of the church such as priests and vicars.

congregation Religious believers gathered together to take part in worship.

cruciform This means shaped like a cross.

denomination A group of churches within Christianity which follow a set of beliefs and practices, for example the Church of England.

Eucharist One of the names for the service associated with the sharing of bread and wine. The word means 'thanksgiving'.

evangelists The four writers of the Gospels, Matthew, Mark, Luke and John. This word can also be used to describe people who want to spread the message of Christianity to others.

Holy Communion/Mass Names associated with the service in which the sharing of bread and wine among the congregation takes place.

hymns Songs that are written to worship or thank God.

Last Supper The Passover meal which Jesus shared with his Disciples on the night before his death.

liturgy The order of a church service.

Mary The mother of Jesus, often referred to as the Blessed Virgin or the Virgin. She is classed as a saint by many Christians.

prayer Way of communicating with God to develop a personal relationship with him.

rosary This word refers to the set of prayers, including the Hail Mary, or the set of prayer beads themselves.

sermon A talk given by the leader of a church service, often to provide an interpretation of the Bible readings or Church beliefs.

stoup A small sink or bowl containing holy water.

transubstantiation The belief that during the service of Holy Communion, the bread and wine are changed into the body and blood of Jesus Christ.

worship A way of celebrating belief in God, giving thanks and praising him.

FOR INTEREST Did you know that the oldest church in Britain that is still used for worship is St Martin's church in Canterbury? The church dates from 597 CE and was used by St Augustine when he arrived from Rome to spread the word of Christianity to the English people. Although there would have been Christians in Britain before this time this is the only church from that time that is still in use today. There may well have been other churches built before then as the Roman Empire was Christian from the time of the Emperor Constantine in 313 CE, but they are no longer standing.

Where and why do Christians worship?

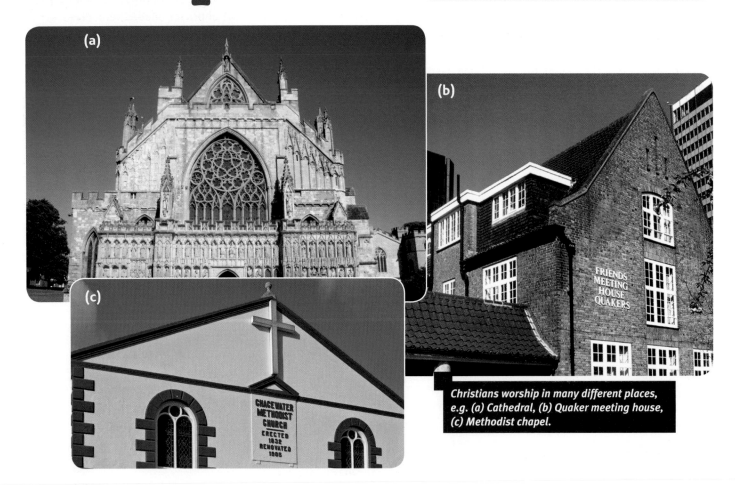

Christians worship in many different places, e.g. (a) Cathedral, (b) Quaker meeting house, (c) Methodist chapel.

Worship

In today's world people might be said to worship many things. We often see, or hear, the phrase 'hero worship' which tends to mean that a person holds another person, often a celebrity, up as a role model or someone to be followed. Some people might be said to worship a football or rugby team.

In the same way, when Christians speak of worshipping, what they mean is that they are giving respect to someone whom they feel is worthy of that respect and that person is God. When Christians worship they are showing respect and appreciation for God and demonstrating how important he is in their lives. They will often worship as a way of saying 'thank you' for all he has done for them.

Worship provides a way of feeling closer to God and developing the relationship that Christians have with him. Worship can also provide peace and reflection time for Christians to think about what really matters in their lives.

The ways in which Christians worship vary. Sometimes they will worship alone or at other times they will worship alongside other members of their community. They may do this at home or in a special place of worship. Sometimes it will take the form of a special ceremony or service and at others it will be a moment of quiet reflection.

The word 'church'

The Christian place of worship is called a church but the word church can be used in three ways. First it describes the whole community of Christians, secondly it describes the building in which Christians worship and thirdly it refers to a particular **denomination**. Today we use the word in all three ways.

You will often find the word used to describe a denomination, for example the Church of England or the Roman Catholic Church. When used in this way it describes the group of believers rather than the building they worship in. The early Christians did not meet in a special place to worship so the word was originally used to describe the group of followers and Jesus used the word in this way.

> **Matthew 16:18**
> *'And I tell you that you are Peter, and on this rock I will build my church'.*

This is how Jesus used the word church. Jesus was talking to the Apostle Simon who from that moment was known as Peter, or Simon Peter, as the word Peter means 'rock'. In Aramaic (the language used by Jesus) the word would have actually been 'cephas'. He was asking Peter to be the foundation of the new church who would be his followers.

Other Christian places of worship

The images on this spread show that not all Christian places of worship are called a church. Other names include chapel, cathedral and meeting house among others. In this book we often use the term church to mean any place of Christian worship.

The purpose of a place of worship is to provide a space for believers to come together as a group to worship. There will usually be set times for formal worship such as **the Eucharist** to take place and these will be displayed on a board outside the building. At other times, Christians may visit the church to worship privately.

Not all Christian worship takes place in a special building. Most Christians will worship at home as well as in a church. Sometimes Christians will gather together in their homes to worship as a group and at other times they will worship alone. In fact, Christian worship can take place at any time or place.

ACTIVITIES

Find or draw a map of your local area. Think about the buildings in it, for example the library or the local shops. Can you identify any churches or other places of worship? List or draw these, on or alongside your map. Count how many there are in your area and compare this number with those of your classmates. Are you surprised by how many there are? Which denominations do they belong to?

REMEMBER THIS

When we use the word church to describe a building we use a small 'c'. When it is used to describe a group of believers, for example a denomination such as the Roman Catholic Church, we use a capital 'C'.

ACTIVITIES

Can you think of any advantages of having a special place to worship? Are there any advantages to worshipping more privately? What do you think a Christian would say to these questions? Role play an interview with a Christian answering these questions and present it back to your class.

What does a church look like?

The next two pages will help you to:

- identify some of the most common features outside churches and other Christian places of **worship**
- compare and contrast some features of different Christian places of worship.

What would you expect to see outside a church?

Churches vary in design and size. Some are ornate with lots of decorative features while others are more modest. Some are huge, designed to accommodate thousands of believers, while others may only hold a small community. Some are old, having been built hundreds of years ago, while others are built in a very modern style. How can you tell a **church** apart from other buildings? The answer is that sometimes you can't. Not all churches have been designed as places of worship. Some churches are buildings that have been converted from other uses, for example a house might have been made into a small church or meeting house. Equally, today some former churches and chapels have been converted into houses, offices or even places of worship for other religions.

Early churches

The earliest Christians did not worship in a special building. The earliest followers of Jesus were Jews and they worshipped in synagogues and homes, as well as in the Temple in Jerusalem. Once Christianity became a separate movement and began to spread, Christians would have met together wherever they could be safe. In Rome, there is evidence that this would have involved meeting in catacombs. Catacombs were burial places under the city.

Christians would have used these to avoid being caught as Christianity was illegal under the Romans until the time of the Emperor Constantine. It was only in 260 or 261 CE that Christians were legally allowed to own property. One of the first churches was probably built on the site of St Peter's grave in Rome where the present Basilica of St Peter stands today. There is little archaeological evidence of the earliest churches but eventually a design emerged which developed into the features we might see today.

AO1 skills

ACTIVITIES

You have been asked to design a new church. As the architect, what features would you make a priority? What materials would you use? How would you decorate the building? Make a sketch of your building or draw a plan of the layout and label your key features. Be prepared to explain your choices.

A typical English village church.

Examples of churches

A typical English village church

This is a traditional village church. It belongs to the Church of England. It has a tower with bells which will be rung to remind people of services or to celebrate festivals such as Christmas or for special occasions such as weddings. The bells also ring to indicate the time to the people of the community. On top of the tower, or spire of a church, is usually a cross to show that this is a holy place for Christians. It has a churchyard where people are buried. The churchyard is surrounded by a wall. The wall indicates the boundary of the church. In times past this represented that the church and the churchyard was a place of sanctuary where God's laws applied and not state laws. There is often a covered gate into the churchyard which is called a 'lychgate'. There may also be large yew trees in the churchyard to symbolise long life. The church has large windows made of stained glass showing scenes from the Bible and images of Jesus and the saints.

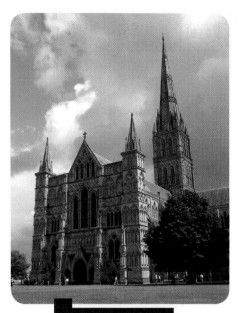

Salisbury Cathedral.

Salisbury Cathedral

This building was completed in 1258. Many cathedrals, such as Salisbury, share some common features of a church, such as large stained glass windows, spires and arched doorways. The outside of Salisbury Cathedral is decorated with 67 statues showing Jesus, **Mary** and other saints. These remind worshippers of the examples that they should follow in their own lives. The size and complexity of the design of this church show its importance to Christians. A cathedral is the seat of a bishop or archbishop.

The Metropolitan Cathedral of Christ the King in Liverpool

The Roman Catholic Cathedral in Liverpool is built in a more modern style. It is circular in shape to allow people to see each other more easily and to provide a central focus on God. Many churches are now built in this shape to allow people to feel closer to each other and to God. Outside you can also see that there are cross-shaped decorations to mark out the building as a Christian place of worship. The building also still retains a more traditional tower.

Metropolitan Cathedral of Christ the King, Liverpool.

An Orthodox church

St Basil's Cathedral is an Orthodox church in Moscow. Notice that the design is very ornate and has lots of decorative features, such as the domes, cupolas (small domes) and a steeple. The domes remind followers that God is above humans and as they stand so high they make the church visible from a long distance away. Orthodox churches are often richly decorated inside as well as being highly coloured.

Other Christian places of worship

Churches do not have to be specially built to a specific design. Many Christians worship in buildings that were not originally designed to be churches. The Religious Society of Friends or 'Quakers' call their places of worship 'Friends' Meeting Houses'.

St Basil's Cathedral, Red Square, Moscow.

Inside a church

What would you expect to see inside a church?

Think about your home. The outside of your home might look much like any other building in the street. Now step inside. Like the other houses in the street it will have a kitchen, a bathroom and some bedrooms. But the inside of your home will be different from the other houses in the street. It will be unique to your family. The decor, the furniture and the personal items such as photographs reflect your family, the way it lives, who is in it and what they find important.

The inside of a **church** building is like this. No two churches are the same inside though they may share some features in common. The inside of a church reflects the people who use it, the way they use it and what they believe is important.

This Topic looks at some features of a typical Church of England church. The Church of England is a Protestant **denomination** and belongs to the worldwide Anglican Church. The leader of the Anglican Church is the Archbishop of Canterbury. Church of England churches can be found in most English towns and villages. Many of their features are shared with churches of many other denominations. The following sections of this book will look at churches from other denominations but many will also share the features here.

Features of a typical church

Many churches are built in the shape of a cross. This shape is called a **cruciform** shape. The steeple, or tower, of the church is positioned above the centre of the cross. To either side are small chapels. The church is usually orientated to face east, towards the rising sun. The eastern end of the church may be semi-circular and is called the apse. In many churches there are a series of small steps which ascend towards the eastern end of the church to show that the areas of the church become more holy as people walk through it towards the altar.

The next two pages will help you to:

- identify some of the most common features inside a Church of England church
- make links between the features of the church and some key beliefs held by Christians
- connect some features of your own life and experiences with those of Christians.

AO1 skills ACTIVITIES

Choose a room in your own house and list or draw the items in it. Label the items and explain what this shows about what is important to the people who live in the house and use this room.

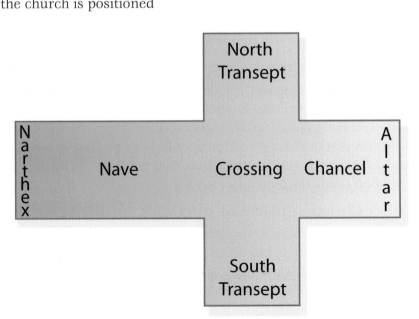

Inside the church

Features inside a church include:

East window: a window is often placed at the eastern end of the church so that it is in the direction of the rising sun which brings light and life to the church. It is usually made of stained glass. The images will show scenes from the Bible and the lives of the saints, especially the saint after whom the church is named.

Altar: this is a table where the bread and wine are blessed during Holy Communion or Eucharist services.

Choir stalls: many church services will include the singing of songs or hymns which are performed by a choir. This area is where the choir sit during the services.

Cross: the empty cross reminds people of Jesus' death and his resurrection.

Font: contains the holy water used for performing baptisms.

Lectern: a stand upon which the Bible is placed to be read from during services.

Nave: the central section of the church. It has an aisle running down the middle of it where people will walk into the church to get to the pews.

Organ: churches often have an organ on which music is played to accompany the choir.

Pews: seats where the **congregation** will sit or kneel during services.

Pulpit: where the priest or minister preaches sermons from. It may have stairs up to it so that the congregation can see and hear more easily.

In many churches you will find flowers, candles and incense. Flower arrangements might be used to decorate the altar and the chapels. Flowers enhance the beauty of the church building. On Easter Sunday there may be special flower arrangements to represent life and the glory of God, celebrating this important day in the Christian calendar.

Candles may be found on the altar, in chapels and near to statues or the cross. People may light them as a sign of remembrance or thanks. They add to the peaceful atmosphere of the church and symbolise light and life.

Incense is a sweet-smelling spice which is burned in churches to create a pleasant aroma. As it burns the smoke wafts upwards, symbolising prayers going up to God.

1 Altar	2 Choir stalls	3 Cross	4 East window	5 Font
6 Lectern	7 Nave	8 Organ	9 Pews	10 Pulpit

John 8:12

When Jesus spoke again to the people, he said, 'I am the light of the world. Whoever follows me will never walk in darkness, but will have the light of life.'

 ACTIVITIES

We often associate our feelings with certain smells. Incense is the same for Christians. What thoughts do you think it would inspire for them? How do you think it makes them feel? How might this help Christians to **worship**?

Inside a Roman Catholic church

The next two pages will help you to:

- identify some of the most common features of the inside of a Catholic church
- make links between features of the **church** and key beliefs held by Roman Catholic Christians.

What would you expect to see in a Roman Catholic church?

The Roman Catholic **Church** is the largest **denomination** of Christianity in the world. There are Catholic churches in almost every country and in Britain today you will find a Catholic church in most towns and cities. Can you think of where the closest Roman Catholic church to your school is situated?

Features of a typical Roman Catholic church

What you would expect to see inside a Roman Catholic church? Although churches vary even within denominations, there are some features which would enable you to tell that a church is a Roman Catholic church.

Holy water stoup

The holy water **stoup** is situated near the entrance to the church, often close to the doors. It is a small sink or bowl which is usually built into the wall of the building and is made of stone. It contains holy water. This means that it has been blessed by the parish priest. As followers enter and exit the church they will pass by the holy water stoup and dip their fingers into the water. They will then make the sign of the cross. As they go into the church it reminds them of the fact that they are entering into God's presence. As they leave it reminds them that they are going back out into the world as Christians.

Crucifix

Roman Catholic churches tend to display a cross with an image of Jesus upon it. This reminds followers of Jesus' sacrifice. The crucifix will often be centrally placed behind the altar and is a main focus during services.

The 6th Station of the Cross – St Veronica wipes the face of Jesus – shown in 'The Procession to Calvary' c.1505 by Ridolfo Ghirlandaio.

 **ACTIVITIES**

Create a leaflet welcoming people to a Roman Catholic church and explaining the importance of some of its key features. If you have access to a computer you might wish to add images to your leaflet or draw them yourself. If you have time you could even visit your local Roman Catholic church and include some of the features you see there.

Statues

Around the church you would expect to see a number of statues. These will be of Jesus, his mother **Mary** and other saints. Statues remind believers of important people and events but they are also symbolic and express key beliefs.

Many churches are named after Mary and Roman Catholics will often pray to her. This **prayer** is known as the Hail Mary (see right).

Statues of the Virgin Mary help believers to understand who Mary was and why she is important to their Christianity. She is often shown with her arms outstretched welcoming followers which demonstrates her caring nature and that the Church welcomes everyone to become members of it. She is also shown holding the infant Jesus. This shows her role as the mother of Jesus.

Some images and statues will also picture her rising into Heaven. Roman Catholics believe that just like Jesus, Mary ascended directly into Heaven. This is known as the Assumption of Mary and this event is celebrated on 15 August each year.

Other statues within the Roman Catholic church might include an image of the saint after whom the church itself was named. For example if a church is named St Mark's then the building would usually have a statue of St Mark displayed within it. St Mark might also appear in pictures or in any stained glass windows which decorate the church.

The Stations of the Cross

On the walls of a Roman Catholic church are displayed a set of engravings or pictures called the Stations of the Cross. They may be made of wood, stone or even metal. These images show the key scenes in the trial and death of Jesus.

There are usually 14 stations around the church and Christians will use the stations to perform their own 'pilgrimage' following in the footsteps of Jesus and using the images to remember the suffering and sacrifice of Jesus. They will pray and meditate at each station. On Good Friday the Priest will lead the whole **congregation** in performing the Stations of the Cross together.

Tabernacle

This is a decorated box sometimes set into the eastern wall at the end of the church. It contains the bread used in the Mass. Once the bread has been blessed, it is regarded as the body of Jesus and so this area is the most holy in the church.

> **The Hail Mary**
>
> *Hail Mary full of grace,*
> *The Lord is with thee,*
> *Blessed art thou among women and*
> *blessed is the fruit of thy womb Jesus,*
> *Holy Mary, Mother of God,*
> *Pray for us sinners now*
> *And at the hour of our death*
> *Amen*

REMEMBER THIS

The Hail Mary forms part of the process of performing the **rosary**. This is a set of prayers that Roman Catholics (and some other Christians) will recite. As they do so they will use a set of beads to help them to concentrate but also to count the number of times that they have said the prayer. The word 'rosary' is used to describe both the set of prayer beads used to help prayer and the saying of the prayers themselves.

According to tradition, St Dominic was given the first rosary by the Virgin Mary in 1214.

Inside an Orthodox church

Orthodox churches look quite different on the inside from the churches considered so far in this Topic. They may also look quite different on the outside as you can see in Topic 4.2. The word Orthodox means 'right', 'true' or 'traditional'. Orthodox churches have a long tradition of **worship** and their churches reflect this.

The next two pages will help you to:

- identify some of the most common features inside an Orthodox **church**
- make links between features of the church and key beliefs held by Orthodox Christians
- explore the similarities and differences between churches of different **denominations**.

The interior of an Orthodox church

Although Orthodox churches may be built in a cross or **cruciform** shape, they can often be built in a rectangular shape.

Orthodox churches follow the tradition of having a special area which is considered holy and which is separated off from the main part of the church. This is called the sanctuary and is divided off by the use of a screen called an Iconostasis.

The Iconostasis

This screen divides the main part of the church, the nave, from the sanctuary area which contains the altar. The screen is usually made of wood, is heavily decorated and does not reach the ceiling to allow the prayers and chanting of the Priests to be heard by the **congregation**. It is divided into three sections.

The middle section has a large door, or doors, called the Holy Door or the Royal Gates. These may include images of Jesus, the four **Evangelists** (Matthew, Mark, Luke and John), the **annunciation** and of the **Last Supper**.

The two sections on either side of the Royal Gates may also have doors on them. These are called the North and South doors. These two sections of the screen will be decorated with images of the saints and the angels.

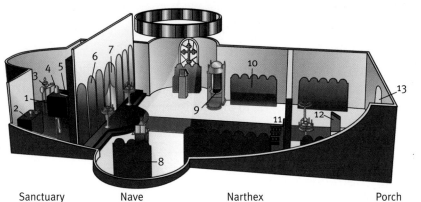

Sanctuary   Nave   Narthex   Porch

1 Altar   2 Table of preparation
3 Exiptera   4 Tabernacle
5 Gospel book   6 Deacon's Doors
7 Beautiful Gates   8 Choir
9 Bishop's Throne   10 Stacidia
11 Royal Doors   12 Icon stand
13 Entrance

The iconostasis of an Orthodox church.

 MUST THINK ABOUT!

Look at the picture of iconostasis used in Orthodox churches. They are often described as 'windows' which allow the believer to see beyond them, towards God. What do you think this means? Discuss this idea of the image as a window with a partner and try to explain it in your own words.

Icons

Orthodox churches are often vividly colourful. Much of this colour and light comes from icons placed around the building. Icons are two-dimensional images or paintings and are often decorated with gold leaf so that they appear to be lit up. The images represented on the icons are often of Jesus or **Mary**, though sometimes they can be of other saints or scenes from the Bible.

Domes

Orthodox churches will often have domes which rise high above the Iconostasis. The dome helps sound to pass from the sanctuary into the nave and also reminds believers of God, high above them. Domes provide an additional surface for beautiful paintings and images which enhance the atmosphere of the church, reminding the congregation of the special nature of the building.

Other features

During services the priests will sing or chant but there will be no music to accompany this as Orthodox churches do not have an organ. There may be very few chairs to sit on in the nave. The members of the congregation are expected to stand during the services. The chairs are only for those who really need them. Both candles and incense are commonly used in Orthodox churches.

 **REMEMBER THIS**

The idea of a sanctuary dates back to the time of Jesus where the Temple in Jerusalem had an area called the Holy of Holies which was considered sacred. Only the High Priest was allowed into this area.

 **ACTIVITIES**

From your reading so far, choose two denominations within Christianity and draw up a table with two columns headed 'Similarities' and 'Differences' to compare their features inside a church.

 GradeStudio

AO1

QUESTION
Describe two features of a place of worship and explain their importance. **[6 marks]**

This is an AO1 question, meaning it is trying to test your knowledge and understanding. Examiners will use three levels to measure how successfully you demonstrate these skills. Let's now look at what you need to do to achieve a higher level

First of all choose two features which have clear religious importance. This might be practical or spiritual importance or even location in the building. You may not be able to say as much about one feature as the other, but this does not matter as your response will be marked by levels; examiners will judge the whole response and not break it into two responses of 3 marks each. You could respond in this way.

Level 1
The font and the altar are two features of many churches. The font is a vessel into which water is poured

and blessed to be used in baptism. The altar is a special table usually set in front of the congregation.

Level 2
To move up to this level, you need to give more detail and a deeper explanation. For example, develop the descriptions by reference to location: in the case of the font, near the door of the church as a symbol of welcoming the person to be baptised into the faith; and to use, in the case of the altar, as the table where the **Eucharist** is prepared and celebrated.

Level 3
Finally, develop the importance of each feature by referring to how the feature shows a key Christian belief: the altar, for example, as symbolic of the table at the Last Supper and of the sacrifice of Jesus, which is celebrated in the Eucharist; the font as the place of baptism, entry into the family of the church and containing the water, symbolic of cleansing from sin.

Inside a Nonconformist church

Nonconformist Churches are often known as the Free Churches. The word nonconformist means rejecting rules and traditions. There are many churches that can be described as Nonconformist.

This Topic will examine the Baptist Church, the Methodist Church and the Religious Society of Friends.

The next two pages will help you to:

- identify how Nonconformist churches may differ from other churches
- make links between the features of Nonconformist churches and their beliefs.

An adult Baptism by total immersion.

The Baptist Church

The key feature of a Baptist church is the area for the performing of baptisms. This is known as the baptistry. It takes the form of a pool which is usually covered and situated near the front of the church. It is only filled with water when it is to be used. Followers of the Baptist Church believe that people should only be baptised when they are old enough to choose to do so. This form of baptism is known as believer's baptism. When being baptised the person is fully immersed in the water for a brief moment.

A Baptist church may share some of the traditional features that are associated with churches of other **denominations**. There will be a pulpit from which the minister who leads services will give his or her

sermon. There will also be a lectern. However, instead of an altar, Baptist churches will have a table at the front called the Lord's Table on which the bread and wine are placed.

The Methodist Church

Methodist churches are simply decorated, reflecting Methodist belief in following a simple but religious life. They share some features in common with Baptist churches. They will have a Lord's Table, a pulpit and a lectern for example. These are at the front of the main area of the church but not separated from it.

The leader of a Methodist church is called a Minister and he or she will perform Baptisms and Communion services but everyone is encouraged to take part in other forms of service. Services may follow a set format laid out in a service book, or may focus on preaching or Bible reading as members of the community take the opportunity to lead them. This emphasises the fact that Methodists believe that everyone is equal in the eyes of God.

The Religious Society of Friends

The Religious Society of Friends are commonly known as the Quakers. They do not call themselves a Church but instead use the term Society. Similarly they do not call their place of **worship** a church but instead use the phrase Meeting House. Followers are called Friends.

Within the Meeting House, the chairs are organised so that they face each other. There is always a table but this is not used for bread and wine as Quakers do not hold any form of Communion service. The table will usually have some flowers on it, alongside a copy of the Bible and a copy of the book *Quaker Faith and Practice*. Meetings often take place in complete silence and meditation. At other times, the Elders may choose to speak but anyone can speak if they feel moved to do so.

MUST THINK ABOUT!

Do you ever sit in silence? In today's world even when we are quiet there are often lots of other noises going on around us. Can you think of any benefits to sitting quietly? How might it make you feel? Can you think why Quakers might use this as a form of worship?

Worship in a Friends Meeting House.

ACTIVITIES

The table below lists some features of Nonconformist churches. Copy and complete the table to match which denomination it is a feature of and what you think the feature tells you about what they believe.

Feature	Denomination	Belief represented
Chairs face each other		
Lord's Table		
Baptistry		
Lack of decoration		
Pulpit and lectern		

Public acts of worship 1

The next two pages will help you to:

- identify and describe the service of the **Eucharist**
- explain why this service is important to Christians.

Young people making their first communion.

What happens inside a church?

There are many ways in which Christians express their beliefs through **worship** in a **church**. There are two reasons for this:

1. There are so many different denominations within Christianity and each has its own beliefs about how worship should take place.

2. Jesus left very few instructions with his Disciples about how they should worship when he was no longer with them.

As a result what takes place in one church will differ from that in another church, sometimes even if they belong to the same **denomination**. Worship that takes place within a church usually involves the members of the community coming together to worship publicly, as a group.

Although there is variation, two features that are common to almost all churches is that worship takes place on a Sunday and there is an emphasis on Jesus throughout as a focal point.

Why Sunday?

Although it is common today to think that the week starts on a Monday, it is traditional for the first day of the week to be a Sunday. In Genesis it says that it was on this day, the first day, that God commanded that there be light. Christians remember this on a Sunday. Sunday was also the day that Jesus rose from the dead following his crucifixion. This makes it an important day to Christians.

Why Jesus?

Although Christians do worship God directly, a key belief of Christianity is that Jesus is the 'Son of God'. Jesus is God as he is part of the Trinity. But Jesus was also a man and a way for Christians to know God. Because of this Christians will worship God through Jesus.

Sunday services

The times at which worship will take place in a church will be displayed on a board outside the church. Some will have more services than others.

Eucharist/Holy Communion

Many Christian services include the sharing of bread and wine amongst the **congregation**. Usually these services follow a set pattern. The word for this is **liturgy**. Each Church has its own form of service book which is used to give an order to the worship that takes place. This will include the prayers, blessings, Bible readings and **hymns** that will be included in the service. However the main focus is the sharing of the bread and wine.

This type of worship is one that is important to many forms of Christianity. It is called the **Eucharist**. Other common names for this type of service are **Holy Communion** or **Mass**. They are centred on the **Last Supper**.

Christians remember the Last Supper because it was the last meal that Jesus shared with the Disciples before his death. He gathered them together to celebrate the Passover meal which is an important festival within Judaism. During the meal he took bread, blessed it and shared it with the Disciples. He then shared a cup of wine with the Disciples.

After Jesus' death, his Disciples continued to meet together and celebrate a meal like this where they remembered Jesus and what he had meant to them. Christians have continued this practice ever since. In taking part in a service in a church where bread and wine are shared, Christians are following in this tradition but what does it mean?

Christians disagree on the meaning. For some Christians, the sharing of the bread and wine is symbolic and is simply a way of remembering Jesus. For others, such as Roman Catholics, when the priest performs the blessings over the bread and wine it actually becomes the body and blood of Jesus and he is spiritually present in the church. This process is known as **transubstantiation**.

Christians would agree that in taking part in this type of service they are remembering Jesus' death and sacrifice but they are also remembering his resurrection. It provides a chance to connect with God.

ACTIVITIES

Think of a meal that you share regularly with your family or friends and that you really enjoy. Now answer the following questions:

1 Who is present at the meal?
2 What do you eat?
3 What is it that makes the meal memorable?
4 Why do you repeat it?

Think about whether there are any similarities between your responses and those that a Christian might give in response if they were asked these questions about taking part in a Eucharist service.

Luke 22:19–20

And [Jesus] took bread, gave thanks and broke it, and gave it to them, saying. 'This is my body given for you; do this in remembrance of me.' In the same way, after the supper he took the cup [of wine], saying 'This cup is the new covenant in my blood, which is poured out for you.'

Public acts of worship 2

Readings from the Bible are an important part of most Christian services.

 **ACTIVITIES**

Design a questionnaire to help you find out more about Christian worship in churches. Think about the kinds of questions raised during this Topic and write these down. You might want to ask these questions to a number of Christians that you know. You could even visit a place of worship to see these activities take place or arrange to speak to a member of the Church to ask them.

What happens inside a church?

There are many features of **worship** in a **church**, both public and more private, that help Christians to express their feelings about God.

Bible reading and Bible services

Taking part in **Eucharist** services in which bread and wine are shared amongst the **congregation** is one way in which Christians worship in a church. Many **denomination**s offer these types of service but not all do. They may choose to offer Bible services as well as, or instead of, Holy Communion.

Bible services may follow a set order of service or may be less structured. The emphasis is on the reading of the Bible. A more structured service would include readings from the Bible but will also include **hymns**, prayers and a **sermon**. The person in charge of the service, usually a minister, will spend time choosing these and explaining the meaning of them to the congregation.

In some churches, for example Pentecostal churches, services may be much less formal. In these services, followers may be encouraged to take part whenever they feel they would like to. The minister will be there to guide the service along but everyone can be a part of the service if they wish to. In some services of this kind, there will be lots of hand-clapping and singing, sometimes even dancing.

Music

One way in which Christians express their belief in God is through the use of music and song. Songs sung in church which are written to express a person's belief in God are called hymns. Many churches have special seated areas for a choir to sit during services. In traditional church buildings these are often found close to the altar and may even be screened off from the rest of the worshippers. In more modern buildings, the choir is often set up high towards the back of the church to enable the sound of the choir to carry through the building.

Many hymns are based on the Psalms which are a collection of poems in the Bible. For example the hymn 'The Lord's my shepherd' is based on Psalm 23.

The instruments used to accompany the singing may vary. Traditional churches often have organs to create a powerful sound. Bands featuring guitars, tambourines and drums are not uncommon in Nonconformist churches where the style of music reflects a less formal approach.

Music can be used to raise spirits in a joyful expression of praise and thanksgiving or it may be used to aid reflection and create a more solemn atmosphere.

Actions

In churches there are a number of ways in which Christians use actions to express something they believe.

At certain points in a church service some Christians will make 'the sign of the cross' which means that they will make a cross with their right hand across their bodies, usually from their forehead, down to their chest and then across each shoulder as a simple reminder of Jesus' death.

Kneeling is another common feature of church worship. This is a sign of respect and is often done in front of the altar. Alternatively some Christians will bow their heads for the same reason.

The shaking of hands as a 'sign of peace' is another feature of some services. Believers will shake hands and say to others nearby 'Peace be with you'. This shows the belief that all members of the church are a part of a community and care for each other.

Silence and meditation

In many services there will be time for quiet reflection and meditation. This allows the believers to contemplate the meaning of the words they have heard or the service they have taken part in. It provides personal thinking time. Some Christians will use this to reflect on their own actions and behaviour, others may use it to simply focus on God.

The Lord's My Shepherd

The Lord's my shepherd, I'll not want;
He makes me down to lie
In pastures green; he leadeth me
The quiet waters by.

My soul he doth restore again,
And me to walk doth make
Within the paths of righteousness,
E'en for his own name's sake.

Yea, though I walk in death's dark vale,
Yet will I fear no ill:
For thou art with me, and thy rod
And staff me comfort still.

My table thou hast furnished
In presence of my foes;
My head thou dost with oil anoint
And my cup overflows.

Goodness and mercy all my life
Shall surely follow me;
And in God's house for evermore
My dwelling-place shall be.

(Scottish Psalter, 1650)

AO1 skills ACTIVITIES

Read the words of the hymn 'The Lord's my shepherd' and then consider the beliefs contained in the quotes below.

The Lord's my shepherd

Yea, though I walk in death's dark vale, Yet will I fear no ill: For thou art with me.

Prayer

Hands by Albrecht Dürer.

The next two pages will help you to:

- explain what **prayer** is
- give examples of the reasons Christians pray.

What is prayer?

Prayer is a way in which Christians try to communicate with God. The ways in which Christians do this are many and varied. It may be an internal conversation which Christians will have with God, it may take the form of a traditional prayer; it may be a spoken prayer or it may be silent. All forms of prayer are ways in which Christians aim to develop their own personal relationship with God.

Jesus did not give his Disciples many instructions regarding how they should pray. He himself attended the synagogue to **worship** alongside other Jews. When asked how people should pray Jesus responded that they should pray behind closed doors and, when alone, in secret. Many Christians spend time praying in this way. Jesus also famously gave his followers the Lord's Prayer.

Most Christians will pray in **church** alongside their fellow believers. Prayer is a central part of church services and many would include the Lord's Prayer. Over the years other prayers have been written down which express Christian beliefs. Anglicans use a book called 'Common Worship' which contains these. Reading the Bible is also a form of prayer.

AO1 skills **ACTIVITIES**

The Lord's Prayer is one that almost all Christians will know off by heart and use. It contains some key beliefs about God. Read the prayer through and discuss with a partner what you think each line is saying about what Christians believe. Now write your own version in a more modern style. You could even try this in 'txt' language. Share what you have done with the rest of the class to see the range of styles and interpretations that the class has come up with.

The Lord's Prayer

Our Father in heaven,
hallowed be your name,
your kingdom come,
your will be done,
on earth as in heaven.
Give us today our daily bread.
Forgive us our sins
as we forgive those who sin against us.

Lead us not into temptation
but deliver us from evil.
For the kingdom, the power,
and the glory are yours
now and for ever.
Amen.

Matthew 6:5–6

And when you pray, do not be like the hypocrites, for they love to pray standing in the synagogues and on the street corners to be seen by men. I tell you the truth, they have received their reward in full. But when you pray, go into your room, close the door and pray to your Father, who is unseen. Then your Father, who sees what is done in secret, will reward you.

Types of prayer

There are many reasons why people pray. These could depend on what is happening in a person's life at that time and sometimes people pray for many reasons all at once. At other times they will have a special focus. Some of the most common reasons are:

- **To thank God**: Christians believe that God is responsible for the world around them, He is all-powerful and all-knowing, the creator. Because they believe this Christians will often thank God for the world around them and everything they believe that he has done for them. This type of prayer is also called thanksgiving.

- **To praise God**: this type of prayer recognises that God is beyond human understanding and worthy of worship. It reminds Christians of God's greatness. This type of prayer is also called adoration.

- **To say sorry to God**: when a person feels that they have done something which has gone against what they believe and that they have in some way let themselves and God down, they may pray to say sorry. This type of prayer is called confession.

- **To ask for God's help**: people petition God. When people feel the need for help, perhaps when things have gone wrong for them and they feel God may be able to help them, giving them strength, they will pray in this way. This type of prayer is called Supplication. They may als o ask for his intervention in the world, for example to help someone who is ill. This type of prayer is called Intercession.

AO2 skills ACTIVITIES

Prayers are like poems. They help believers to express what is important to them. Think about what is important to you. This might be your friends, your family, a hobby or a religious belief. Now compose a poem or prayer about what you find important in your life. You might want to keep this private and personal.

  GradeStudio

AO2

QUESTION
Christians should not need a special building for worship.

[12 marks]

Before responding to the statement, identify the key words in it. Here the key words are *should* and *need*. Use a spider diagram to note down all the possible views that you might wish to use. The response could be built up in this way. Examiners use four levels for AO2 which means they can evaluate muddled responses, but it is better to be well organised as that will ensure you reach the highest levels more easily. Let's look at what you need to do to move up to the higher levels.

Level 1
Start by giving a simple statement and explain a point of view for or against the issue, for example Christians worship an invisible God who is everywhere, so he can be worshipped anywhere.

Level 2
Develop the statement and offer some support. Add another point of view for, or against, and develop it, or relate it, to the first point, for example as God can be

worshipped anywhere not only are buildings or special places unnecessary, they are a waste of money which could be spent on other things such as helping the poor.

Level 3
Go on to weigh up arguments against each other and justify them in some depth. Offer another point of view, for example that a building gives a place where Christians can assemble and share their faith. Christianity is not a solitary religion but a community one. Every human community has special buildings which are a physical statement of the community. Give your own view.

Level 4
Finally check that your response is well organised, your arguments have been justified and some comparison has been made between them. Make a clear reference to Christianity and a good use of technical terms. Include your own view, which might be that a special building can aid worship because of its design, features and possibly location. Support this with evidence, for example that the cruciform design of a church reminds worshippers of the sacrifice of Jesus on the cross. Also make sure you have supported your own view.

The role of religious leaders in worship

The next two pages will help you to:

- describe the roles of religious leaders in Christian **worship**
- explore the differences between the roles of religious leaders in different **denominations**.

Many church services are formal occasions which are led by a religious leader. They follow a set format and the leader performs the rites and leads the **congregation** in worship.

The roles and responsibilities of religious leaders differ among the many denominations of Christianity. Some churches have many levels of leader while others have few. For some this is linked to the size of the denomination, but for others this is linked to their beliefs.

In this Topic we will consider some of the main denominations and the religious leaders who lead their worship.

The Anglican Church

In the Anglican Church, which includes the Church of England, church services are usually led by a vicar (this is another term for parish priest). The role of the parish vicar is to lead church services such as the Sunday service or **Eucharist**, and perform baptisms, marriages and funerals. They are also a valuable member of the community, visiting the sick and taking part in charity events to raise money for the community.

The Vicar is the representative of the Church for the parish. Parishes are organized into groups of parishes which are overseen by a Bishop or an Archbishop. All members of the **clergy**, such as Bishops and Archbishops, can perform services. At the moment in the Church of England, Vicars may be male or female but only males can become Bishops and Archbishops.

The Roman Catholic Church and the Orthodox Church

The title 'priest' is commonly used to describe the leader of the worship in the Roman Catholic Church and the Orthodox Church. Just as in the Anglican Church, the priest is the representative of the Church for a parish and will preside over the church services in that area. The priest has the authority to perform religious rites and sacraments. These would include celebrating the **Mass**, and performing ceremonies such as confession and confirmation. In these traditions, the priest must be male. No females are allowed to be members of the clergy. This is because it says in the Bible that women should be quiet in church. Not all Christians agree with this and it is a matter of much debate.

 **ACTIVITIES**

Many organisations, religions included, have hierarchies. Hierarchies are structures which show the different roles that are performed by people at different levels within the organisation. Think about your school and answer the following questions:

- Who is at the top level of the hierarchy?
- How many levels are there?
- Who is at the bottom of the hierarchy?
- Where do you fit?

Now use this information to draw a family tree type diagram showing your school's hierarchy.

Is this an effective method of organisation? What advantages are there to having a hierarchy? Why do you think churches have these?

> **1 Corinthians 14:34**
> *Women should remain silent in the churches. They are not allowed to speak, but must be in submission, as the Law says.*

The Roman Catholic Church is organised into groups of parishes called dioceses. Each of these is led by a bishop. The leader of the Roman Catholic Church in Britain is an archbishop and he belongs to a group of archbishops who are led by the Pope in Rome.

The Orthodox Church also has a hierarchy of bishops which are overseen by a Patriarch. There are five Patriarchs who preside over the cities of Istanbul, Antioch, Alexandria, Jerusalem and Moscow. Unlike the Catholic Church, there is no one leader of the Orthodox Church.

The Methodist Church

In Methodist churches, services are often led by a local preacher. The preacher is not a member of the clergy itself. Members of the clergy are called ministers. They are usually associated with a group of churches in a local area (called a circuit). Ministers move to a different circuit every five years. There is little hierarchy within the Methodist Church, although the circuits are grouped into districts led by a District Chairman. The leading of services by local preachers reflects the more informal approach to worship in a Methodist church.

The Religious Society of Friends

The Religious Society of Friends has no formal hierarchy. At meetings, followers will sit in contemplative silence for much of the time. The meetings end when two Elders shake hands. The Elders are long standing members of the Society. Quakers may or may not choose to speak during the services.

ACTIVITIES

You have been asked to take part in the interview process for a church leader for your local church along with some other members of the local community. Consider the roles that a church leader performs. What characteristics would be most important in such a person? Write a list of questions that you would like to ask the person being interviewed. If you have time, write a set of answers to the questions that you hope the interviewee would respond with or role play the interview with a classmate.

AO1

QUESTION
Explain the importance of religious leaders in worship.
[6 marks]

This is an AO1 question, which is designed to test your knowledge and understanding. Examiners will use three levels to measure how successfully you demonstrate these skills. Let's now look at what you need to do to achieve a higher level.

No specific religious leaders are mentioned in the specification so you have to select one or more and develop your answer accordingly.

Level 1
Identify a leader, and state the denomination. Refer to practical importance: for example, in a Baptist church, the worship is led by a person called the minister who leads the service. He or she will lead the prayers and preach the **sermon**.

Level 2
To move up to this level, you need to give a deeper explanation, for example that the minister has been trained and ordained which means that the church has accepted them and given them the right to guide worship and minister to the congregation in other ways. Ministers are important because during worship they guide the congregation about Christian beliefs and way of life.

Level 3
To reach this level develop the response to refer to the importance of the minister in ensuring that the worship follows the pattern of the denomination, for example that as a Baptist minister he or she will lead the congregation through the **Holy Communion** service in a way that is appropriate to the Baptist view of the Holy Communion. You could also say how the minister helps to focus the attention of the worshippers by planning a coherent service, for example by organising other members of the congregation to take a part in the service. Conclude by stressing that a leader ensures that worship is orderly and prevents groups in the congregation taking control.

Welcome to the Grade Studio

To get high grades in this Topic you will need to have a good knowledge of the structure and content of a place of worship as well as being able to show that you know how, and for what reasons, Christians will use the place, and the artefacts within it, in their public worship.

What sort of questions will you be asked? You can expect to be asked specific factual questions about the artefacts and the symbolic important of the places of worship. You will be expected to be able to describe what goes on in worship and what it means to Christians.

Although you can respond to the questions from the perspective of one group within Christianity, you must know about all the items listed in specification as you could be asked about any of them. An example: How is the lectern used in worship?

Sometimes questions will expect you to select items to write about. If this is the case, make sure you choose ones which have clear religious importance, for example *Explain the importance of two religious features of a church building*. The key word in this question is religious. So how would you answer this question?

Graded examples for this topic

AO1

Question

Explain the importance of two religious features of a church building.   **[6 marks]**

First step: select two items.

Examiner's guidance

> Flying buttresses and spires are not really a good choice of feature. Select features like the altar and pulpit. These are appropriate and not just architectural and you will be able to say a lot about why they are important to believers. Please note, the Vicar or Priest is not a feature of the building! If you select weak examples it will limit the number of marks you could be awarded.

Second step: explain the importance of each feature.

Examiner's guidance

> There may be something you can say as an introduction that is common to both features, but your response will not be marked at a high level if you say both features are important for the same reasons. Again the choice of features is crucial. So both the altar and the pulpit are important because they are used in worship, which is a start, but then you must say why each is important. Location is important for each of these items as well but again you must explain why for each item.
>
> Think of importance in three ways, for worship, for any religious symbolism about the feature and about where it is located in the church building.

Student's answer

Most churches have stained glass windows and crosses. These are important because they bring Christians closer to God because with the windows they see stories from the Bible and the cross reminds them of Jesus.

Examiner's comment

Although these features could be appropriate and there is an attempt at explanation there is very little detail or development.

Student's improved answer

Most parish churches have a pulpit and a font. The pulpit is important from a practical point of view because it is a platform raised up from the congregation which makes it easier for people to see and hear the person giving the sermon. Its position in the church reflects how central the preaching and the Bible as the word of God are in the worship. Baptist churches may have a central pulpit, showing that the Bible and preaching are central to their faith and worship. Anglican churches may have the pulpit set to one side showing the Bible and preaching are important but not as central to worship as the Eucharist which is celebrated on the second feature, the altar. This is a table usually made special by being covered with a rich cloth. It is the focal point of many churches, usually set in the sanctuary which may be higher than the rest of the church. In some churches it has been brought forward, nearer to the congregation. It is important because the bread and wine for Eucharist is prepared and distributed from the altar. It reminds Christians of the sacrifice Jesus made on the cross.

Examiner's comment

This is not a perfect response as there is a great deal more that could be said about each feature. Check back in your notes to see what else could be said. However, in an exam you only have a certain amount of time, so you have to make a selection of what you think are the best things to say.

Before you leave this Topic

Check you can answer the questions below. All of them are AO1.
- How is the lectern used in worship?
- Describe and explain the importance of the location of the Iconostasis in an Orthodox Church.
- Describe how a Christian might worship in private.
- Explain how the design of a church might reflect the beliefs of the worshippers.
- Describe how old fashioned church buildings get in the way of modern Christian worship.

These specimen answers provide an outline of how you could construct your response. Space does not allow us to give a full response. The examiner will be looking for more detail in your actual exam responses.

Remember and Reflect

AO1 Describe, explain and analyse, using knowledge and understanding

Find the answer on:

1 Using your knowledge of churches and denominations, draw and label a floor plan of a typical church of a specific denomination. Include as many features as you can.
> PAGE 85

2 Choose three features that you consider to be most important in a church and explain what they are used for and why this feature is important in Christian worship.
> PAGE 85

3 Identify one feature that is unique to Orthodox churches and explain its purpose.
> PAGE 88, 89

4 Explain the importance of the Eucharist/Holy Communion/Mass.
> PAGE 93

5 Give examples of the reasons Christians will pray to God.
> PAGE 97

6 Explain the purpose of the following features of the outside of a church:
 a tower/steeple b cross c churchyard
> PAGE 83

7 Explain how the word church is used in different ways.
> PAGE 81

8 Describe the role of a Church of England vicar.
> PAGE 98

9 What are the Stations of the Cross in a Roman Catholic church? How are they used?
> PAGE 87

10 What does the word cruciform mean? Why are many churches built in this shape?
> PAGE 84

11 Explain why there are a variety of ways in which Christians worship.
> PAGE 92

12 Give reasons for the presence of the following in many churches:
 a flowers b incense c candles
> PAGE 85

13 Compare a Society of Friends meeting with a church service from another denomination. What features do they have in common? What features make a meeting distinctive?
> PAGE 81

14 Explain in your own words what Jesus meant when he said to the Disciple Simon Peter that he was the 'rock' upon which the church would be built.
> PAGE 81

Bible study is an important part of life for many Christians.

1 'It is not possible to be a Christian without going to church.' Do you agree with this statement? Explain your thinking on this issue.

2 Do you think that all Churches should worship in the same way? Construct a set of arguments for and against this statement.

3 What do you think a Christian would say to the following question: 'Why do you pray?'

4 The following are features of some church services: hymns; a sermon; Bible readings; prayer; Eucharist; sign of peace. Sort these into a list with the most important at the top.

5 Which feature is the most important to Christian worship in your opinion? Justify your thinking.

6 'All people are equal in the eyes of God and therefore there should be no leaders in church.' Do you agree with this statement? Explain your thinking on this issue.

7 'Christians can pray anywhere so there is no need to have a specific building in which to do so.' Construct a paragraph that a Christian might write in response to this statement.

8 Jesus said that his followers should pray behind closed doors and in secret but many Christians worship publicly, in churches. Consider the reasons for and against worshipping publicly and weigh these up to come to a conclusion.

Topic 5: Religion in the faith community and the family

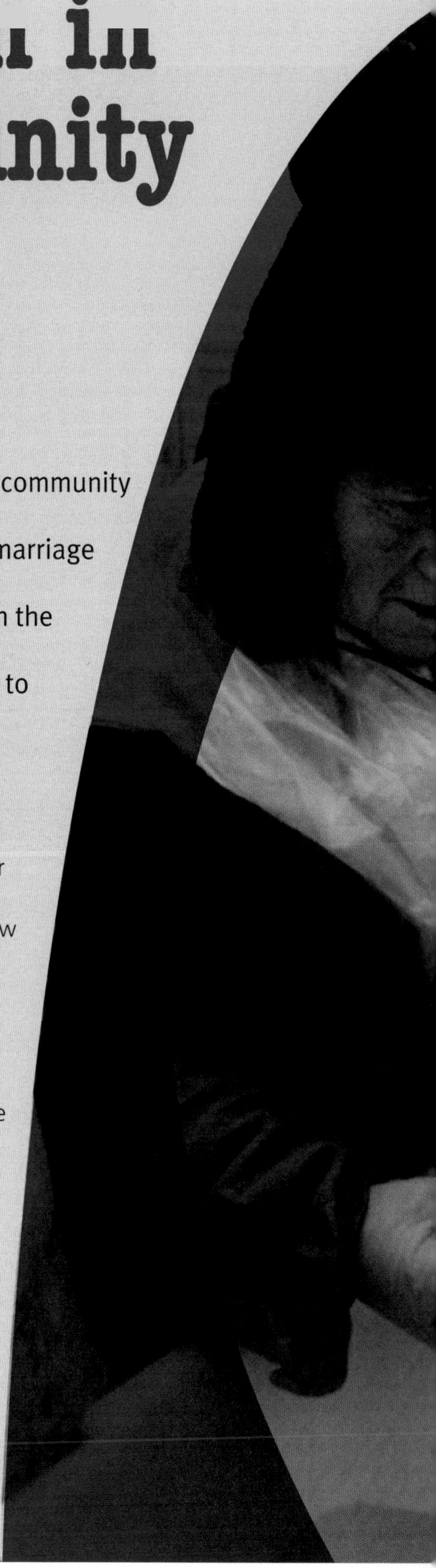

The Big Picture

In this Topic you will examine:

- some of the ways in which Christianity is practised in the faith community and the family
- how rituals are used to mark significant events such as birth, marriage and death
- ways in which beliefs affect the life and outlook of Christians in the world today
- the place of religion in human experience and how this relates to your own experience.

What?

You will:

- develop your knowledge and understanding of key Christian beliefs about rituals and celebrations, commitment, the importance of the family, care for others and membership of the Christian community
- explain what these beliefs and ideas mean to Christians and think about how they might affect how they live
- make links between these beliefs and ideas and what you think/believe.

Why?

Because:

- these beliefs and ideas underpin and are reflected in the ways Christians live their lives, for example, in helping them to decide what principles and values should govern their relationships in the family and wider community and their responsibilities to others
- understanding people's beliefs can help you understand why they think and act the way they do
- understanding these beliefs helps you compare and contrast what others believe, including thinking about your own beliefs and ideas.

How?

By:

- recalling and selecting information about Christian beliefs and ideas, explaining their importance for people today
- thinking about the relevance of these beliefs in 21st-century Britain
- evaluating your own views about these beliefs.

Salvation Army soup kitchen.

⏱ **GET STARTED**

'All Christians have a responsibility to help the poor.' Do you agree or disagree? Give reasons. Do a survey to find out whether people are really concerned about making sure the things they buy, food and clothes for example, have been fairly traded.

Religion in the faith community and the family

Baptism or dedication of an infant

- Most Christian groups have a ceremony to recognise the birth of a baby and welcome the child into their community.

- In the Roman Catholic, Orthodox and Anglican Churches baptism is believed to be a sacrament, an outward visible sign of an inward spiritual grace.

- In infant baptism the priest sprinkles water over the baby's head and makes the sign of the cross.

- In some churches a baby is welcomed in a service of dedication because the members believe baptism has more meaning when a person is older.

Showing commitment to Christianity

- Different branches or denominations of the Church have different ceremonies to show that people want to commit to their faith.

- The Church of England, Roman Catholic and Methodist Churches have a confirmation service when people choose to 'confirm' the promises made on their behalf when they were baptised.

- The Roman Catholic and Orthodox Churches and some Anglicans believe that confirmation is a sacrament.

- In Baptist, Pentecostal and some Evangelical Churches adults are baptised by immersing them in water as a sign that they want to commit their lives to discipleship and the Church.

Christian belief about marriage

- Christians believe marriage is a gift from God and part of God's plan that people should live together, have children and bring them up in a secure, loving Christian environment.

- In a Christian marriage ceremony the couple promise that they will stay together and be faithful to each other for life.

- One of the most popular Bible readings at weddings is about love, from St Paul's first letter to the Christians at Corinth (1 Corinthians 13).

Funeral rites

- Christians believe that death is not the end and that people will be resurrected in either a physical or spiritual form and judged by God for the way they have lived.

- Funerals provide comfort and reassurance for bereaved relatives and friends of the person who has died.

- The 23rd Psalm, 'The Lord is my Shepherd', is often chosen as a reading at Christian funerals.

KNOWLEDGE AND UNDERSTANDING
Choose either marriage or infant baptism and explain how they are celebrated.

ANALYSIS AND EVALUATION
Couples who do not attend church regularly should not be allowed to marry or have their children baptised there. Do you agree? Give reasons and show that you have considered different views.

The nurture of the young and the role of the family

- Christians believe the family was created by God.

- The fifth of the Ten Commandments is that people should honour their father and mother.

- Many churches support family life by running Sunday Schools to teach children about Christianity and to help them live by Christian values.

Christian teaching about charity and concern for others

- Jesus taught about caring for others in the parables of the Sheep and the Goats and the Good Samaritan.

- The Golden Rule teaches that you should treat others as you would like to be treated yourself.

- Christians believe that everything they have has been given to them by God.

The role and significance of religious communities to their members and the wider community

- Tearfund is a Christian group which campaigns to get a fairer deal for the world's poor.

- Many Christians support Christian charities such as Christian Aid.

- Some Christians become monks or nuns and join religious communities which take care of the poor.

FOR INTEREST The number of parents choosing to have their children baptised is declining. Find out what the Church of England is doing to try and encourage young families to come to church.

Religion in the faith community and the family

How rituals affect Christian belief

Events can be like milestones that mark a special place on the journey through life. The most important for many people, as you will probably have discovered from your visit to any card shop, are birth, marriage and death. Every religion regards these as events of great significance, because they raise questions about the meaning and purpose of our existence. They are often marked with special and memorable ceremonies.

Many people choose to live their lives according to a religion and commit themselves to that faith, its beliefs and way of life. There are ceremonies to mark this commitment to a faith. Why are these ceremonies so significant? What do you believe about the aspects of life with which they are concerned?

Baptism

Most Christian Churches (groups, denominations) have a ceremony to recognise the birth of a baby. This may involve the symbolic act of baptism. It is also an occasion when the baby will be named and given its Christian name(s).

Baptism is a way of welcoming a child into the family of the church and starting them on their Christian life. Many Christian parents choose to have their children baptised because they want to bring them up in the Christian faith. Parents choose friends or relatives to be godparents for the child. Their role is to be a good example and help with the Christian upbringing of the child. They make promises on the child's behalf and will pray for them regularly.

Christianity teaches that when Adam and Eve picked and ate the fruit from the Tree of the Knowledge of Good and Evil in the Garden of Eden they disobeyed God and introduced original sin into the world. This means that every child is

> **The next two pages will help you to:**
>
> - identify the features of **baptism** and **dedication**
> - examine the differences between baptism and dedication
> - consider the place of ritual in human experience and how this relates to your own life.

What is the significance of water in baptism?

born with original sin. When a baby is baptised this original sin is washed away and the child is now in a state where, when they die, they could go to Heaven.

The most important part of the baptism is the sprinkling of water from the font on the head of the child. The font is usually near the door of the church to symbolise that baptism is the first step on the journey to becoming a Christian. The parents and godparents answer questions about their faith for themselves and on behalf of the baby. At the end of the baptism service the baby is welcomed into the Church by the members of the congregation.

Infant Dedication

Not all Christian churches baptise babies. Many Nonconformist Churches such as the Baptist Church and the United Reformed Church welcome a new baby into the church in what is called a service of Infant Dedication. This is because they believe that baptism has more meaning when the person is older and can decide for him or herself when they want to be baptised.

It is also based on the belief that adult, rather than infant, baptism was practised by the first Christians in the early Church. There are no godparents but when parents bring their baby to church for the dedication service they are thanking God for the gift of a child and asking their fellow church members to pray that they will be able to fulfil their responsibilities as parents. At this service the child is given its Christian name(s) which has been chosen by the parents.

In a service of Dedication the Minister asks the parents: 'In the name of the Church I ask you: do you acknowledge with gratitude the goodness of God and the gift of this child, and do you accept the responsibility which comes with the gift to give your child a Christian upbringing?' The parents respond by saying 'We do'.

The parents are then asked, 'Will you try to order your home life so that your child will be surrounded by Christian example and influence?' The congregation are then asked to stand and show that they will accept the responsibility to welcome and support the family in whatever ways they can. Prayers are then said asking God to bless the baby and parents. A special certificate is given to mark the occasion.

RESEARCH NOTE

Research the meaning of these words: baptism, Christening, dedication, godparents, Nonconformists, secular.

AO2 skills ACTIVITIES

Which Christian groups practise **infant baptism** and which choose to welcome new babies through a service of dedication? What are the reasons for the difference in their practice?

Identify the similarities and differences between baptism and dedication. What advantages and what disadvantages can you see in each ceremony for the parents and for the child?

Showing commitment to Christianity

The next two pages will help you to:

- examine the concept of commitment in religious and **secular** contexts
- identify the main features of **confirmation** and **believer's baptism**
- analyse the differences between confirmation and believer's baptism
- explore views about commitments.

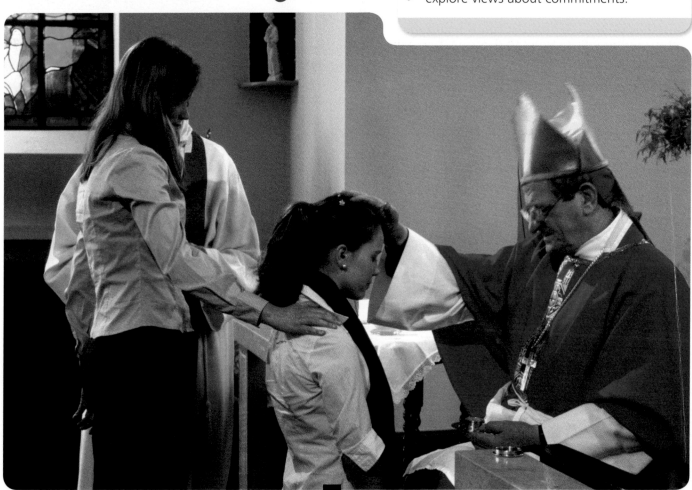

A young person being confirmed by a Bishop.

Commitment to Christianity

In Christianity there are different ceremonies where someone shows commitment to their faith as an adult. The ceremony varies depending on which denomination or branch of the church they belong to. The Roman Catholic, Orthodox, Church of England and Methodist Churches have a ceremony called confirmation while some Nonconformist and Evangelical Churches have believer's baptism.

 **ACTIVITIES**

Look up the account of the Apostles' experience in Acts 2:1–42. Write a letter from one of the Apostles describing what you experienced and how you felt on that day. If you had seven gifts of the spirit to bestow on someone to support them through life what would they be?

What is confirmation and why are people confirmed?

Confirmation means strengthening or deepening one's relationship with God.

When a baby is baptised the parents and **godparents** promise that they will encourage the child to 'confirm' these promises when they are old enough to understand what they mean. Confirmation is a sign that someone has full membership of the Christian community.

There is no set age for confirmation. Some people choose to be confirmed when they are quite young while others decide to wait until they are adults. Churches hold special classes to prepare people for confirmation.

Confirmation has its roots in the teaching of Jesus that, after his death, he would send 'another counsellor' to empower his disciples to bear witness. In the Acts of the Apostles the apostles experience the coming of the Holy Spirit on the day of Pentecost. The person being confirmed believes they are receiving the gift of the Holy Spirit. In the Roman Catholic and Orthodox Churches, confirmations are done at the age of about 14. They are often carried out on Pentecost Sunday when Christians celebrate the coming of the Holy Spirit to the Apostles.

Confirmations are carried out by a bishop in the Church of England, Roman Catholic and Orthodox Churches. The candidates often wear white to symbolise purity of their intention to make a commitment. The bishop lays hands on the head of each candidate and prays that they will receive the seven gifts of the Holy Spirit. These are: reverence, understanding, courage, knowledge, wisdom, awe and wonder, and right judgement.

What is believer's baptism?

Although most Christian groups baptise babies, there are some which believe that because baptism is a commitment to discipleship, and the Church, it can only be meaningful when people are old enough to make this important decision for themselves. The Baptist Church teaches that the baptism of believers was practised by the early Church and that Jesus set an example when he was baptised by John the Baptist at the start of his ministry (Matthew 3:13–17; Mark 1:9–11; Luke 3:21–22).

The Baptist Union of Great Britain teaches that 'to be baptised is a way of opening ourselves to God's blessing and of expressing our commitment to lives as disciples of Christ'. The ceremony of believer's baptism takes place in a **baptistry**, a small pool inside the church, usually at the front.

 **ACTIVITIES**

Think about an example of something you have committed yourself to – it might be a club or a sports activity. What is involved in your commitment? Compare experiences in your class or group and use them to develop a mind map with *Commitment* at the centre. Include branches for *religious commitment* and *secular commitment*, looking for links between them.

 **RESEARCH NOTE**

'Look, here is water. Why shouldn't I be baptised?' (Acts 8:36). Look up this story of Philip, a member of the early church, baptising an Ethiopian he met while travelling. What do you think is the significance of this story in relation to the development and spread of Christianity?

 **ACTIVITIES**

Prepare a script so that you can role play a conversation between two young people. One is a Baptist who has recently been baptised, the other has just been confirmed as a member of the Church of England. They are telling each other why they took this step and what was involved. What are the similarities and differences between their experiences?

Christian beliefs about marriage

A Christian wedding ceremony.

The marriage ceremony

Marriage is important for Christians because they believe it is a gift from God and part of God's plan for creation that men and women should live together. For Roman Catholic and Orthodox Christians and some Anglicans marriage is a sacrament. It provides a relationship through which husband and wife support each other, is built on love and faithfulness, and provides a secure environment for bringing up children. Jesus emphasised the importance of marriage.

> **Mark 10:6–9**
>
> *But at the beginning of creation God made them male and female. 'For this reason a man will leave his father and mother and be united to his wife, and the two will become one flesh.' So they are no longer two, but one. Therefore what God has joined together, let man not separate.*

Most Churches expect the bride and groom to be Christians as they will be making religious statements and promises. It would be considered hypocritical to profess to be Christian simply to have a church wedding. The Marriage Measure, which was published in 2008 by the House of Bishops, includes guidelines that make it easier for people to get married in the Anglican parish where they live or where their family has lived in the past, even if they have limited connections with the church.

The Church of England allows divorce but if divorced people want to remarry it is up to the priest to decide whether they can remarry in church.

What happens in a Christian marriage ceremony?

Christianity teaches that one of the main purposes of marriage is to have children and bring them up in a secure and loving Christian environment so that they will come to love God and follow Jesus.

The wedding ceremony begins with the priest, minister or vicar explaining that marriage is a sacred institution for having children and bringing them up in a Christian family. This is explained by the priest at the start of the Church of England wedding service.

There may be a talk by the vicar/minister and Bible readings about the nature of Christian marriage. Couples frequently choose 1 Corinthians 13 which is about love. The exchange of vows commits the couple to lifetime marriage. They promise that they will be faithful to each other and not have sex with anyone else. Sometimes there is a symbolic binding of the hands in the priest's stole with the words 'Those whom God has joined together let no one put asunder.' The couple exchange rings symbolising the unending nature of marriage. There are prayers asking God's blessing on the couple and the help of God in making the marriage work. At the end of the ceremony the couple and their witnesses sign the register to make the marriage legal.

ACTIVITIES

Look at the vows made at a Christian wedding. Write in your own words exactly what the couple are promising to each other. How difficult do you think it is to keep these promises? Is it reasonable to expect people to stay married for life? Support your views with reasons. Look up 1 Corinthians 13 and make a list of the qualities in verses 4–7 saying for each how they might help a marriage to last. Explain why Christians believe marriage is important.

I, (name), take you, (name), to be my wife, (or husband),
to have and to hold, from this day forward,
for better, for worse,
for richer, for poorer,
in sickness and in health,
to love and to cherish,
till death us do part,
according to God's holy law.
In the presence of God I make this vow.

Funeral rites 1

Funeral rites and Christian beliefs

Although religions have different ways of conducting funeral rites, reflecting their different beliefs, for all religions funerals are an important way of helping to support those who are bereaved. <u>Funerals provide comfort, reassurance and a chance for relatives and friends to say 'Goodbye' and to celebrate the life</u> of the person who has died.

Most of the things Christians do when a person has died are closely linked to what they believe about life after death. Christian funerals vary slightly depending on the denomination to which people belong. Sometimes when someone is dying a priest or minister will come to their bedside to prepare them for death. Prayers will be said and Holy Communion may be celebrated. If the dying person belongs to the Roman Catholic Church the priest will anoint them with holy oil as a preparation for death. Roman Catholic and Orthodox Churches believe that this is a sacrament.

When a person dies their body is placed in a coffin. The coffin may be left open so that relatives can say their final goodbye. The funeral usually takes place about a week later. Often the person will have made clear what their wishes are for their funeral service.

What happens at a Christian funeral?

The priest begins the service by saying 'I am the resurrection and the life. He who believes in me will live, even though he dies; and whoever lives and believes in me will never die.' (John 11:25b–26a)

> **The next two pages will help you to:**
>
> - identify the main features of Christian funeral rituals
> - explore how funeral rites reflect Christian beliefs and aim to support the **bereaved**
> - begin to consider your own views about different ways of coping with death and bereavement.

MUST THINK ABOUT!

What are funerals?
What are they for?
Who are they for?

A coffin is carried into the church for a funeral service.

The priest may then say a few words to comfort the bereaved people. There can be readings from the Bible, such as Psalm 23, which is often chosen, or readings which were chosen by the person who died or by their friends and family. Special music is often played. There is what is called a 'eulogy' when someone talks about the life of the person who has died and the things that they had achieved. The service may also include a time for quiet reflection so that people can think about the person they have lost.

In a Roman Catholic Church a special Eucharist called a Requiem Mass will be held. Prayers will be said for the soul of the person who has died.

After the funeral the body is either cremated or buried. Although many people now choose cremation, burials are still common. They may be in cemeteries or, especially in rural areas, in churchyards, attached to Anglican (Church of England) churches.

Burials and cremations

As the coffin is lowered into the grave the priest or minister recites words from the Bible, for example:

We have entrusted our brother/sister to God's mercy,
and we now commit his/her body to the ground:
earth to earth, ashes to ashes, dust to dust:
in sure and certain hope of the resurrection to eternal life
through our Lord Jesus Christ,
who will transform our frail bodies
that they may be conformed to his glorious body,
who died, was buried, and rose again for us.
To him be glory for ever.
Amen.

As the words 'earth to earth, ashes to ashes, dust to dust' are said a handful of earth is thrown into the grave.

Many Christians choose cremation as a way of disposing of the body. The funeral service is held in a quiet chapel and is similar to the service held at the graveside. When it comes to the time for the committal the priest or minister says: 'We have entrusted our sister/ brother to God's merciful keeping and we now commit her/his body to be cremated, earth to earth, ashes to ashes, dust to dust...'

As these words are spoken a curtain closes quietly around the coffin. After the service is over the coffin is placed in a furnace and the ashes are extracted later. These may be buried or scattered in a place that was special to the person who had died, or in the garden of the crematorium.

The grave or place where the ashes have been interred is usually marked by a gravestone or plaque. The Church of England now has rules about the words that may be written on a gravestone. Apart from the person's name and dates of birth and death, only words which 'express a Christian hope' are permitted.

AO1 skills ACTIVITIES

Read Psalm 23 carefully. Make a list of the words that might provide comfort for someone who is bereaved. What symbols are used? Why do you think it is a popular choice as a funeral reading?

Psalm 23

The Lord is my shepherd, I shall not be in want.
He makes me lie down in green pastures,
he leads me beside quiet waters,
he restores my soul.
He guides me in paths of righteousness
for his name's sake.
Even though I walk
through the valley of the shadow of death,
I will fear no evil,
for you are with me;
your rod and your staff,
they comfort me.
You prepare a table before me
in the presence of my enemies.
You anoint my head with oil;
my cup overflows.
Surely goodness and love will follow me
all the days of my life,
and I will dwell in the house of the Lord
forever.

AO1 skills ACTIVITIES

What do you think might be a suitable 'Christian hope' to place on a gravestone?

Funeral rites 2

The next two pages will help you to:

- explain how funeral rites reflect Christian beliefs and aim to support the **bereaved**
- express your own views about different ways of coping with death and bereavement.

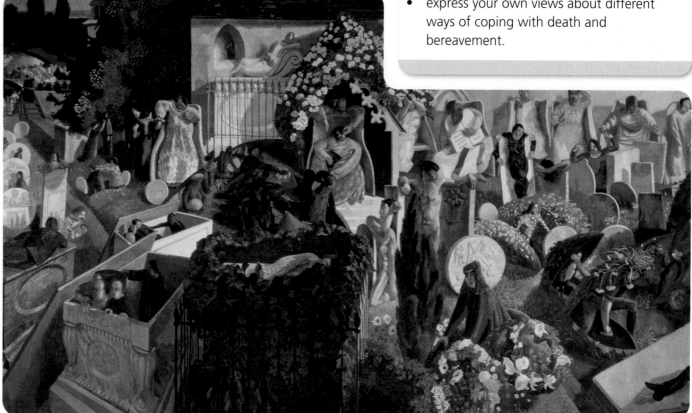

'The Resurrection, Cookham' by Stanley Spencer.

Christians believe that death is not the end. The **Apostles' Creed** states 'I believe… in the resurrection of the body'. Some Christians believe that this means that people will be resurrected in physical form but St Paul said that 'It is sown a natural body, it is raised a spiritual body. If there is a natural body, there is also a spiritual body' (1 Corinthians 15:44).

Many Christians believe in a physical resurrection and that the body stays in the grave until the end of the world when everyone is raised by God. God will then judge everyone and the faithful will go to Heaven and those who have not lived good lives will go to Hell.

The Resurrection, Cookham

This is a very famous painting by Stanley Spencer, an artist who often painted Christian subjects and events but put them in the context of his own 20th-century world. The picture is very big and hangs in the Tate Britain Gallery in London, attracting many visitors. People seem fascinated by it and often spend a long time just looking at it and thinking.

 RESEARCH NOTE

Look at the death notices in your local papers and identify some which clearly express a belief in the resurrection.

 MUST THINK ABOUT!

Suppose a resurrection could happen in the way Stanley Spencer has shown in his painting. How do you feel about this idea? What good things could come from it and what problems might there be?

Spencer frequently included people he knew and loved in his pictures, often as he remembered them when they were happy. In this picture the dead are being resurrected in the churchyard in the village of Cookham, Berkshire, where Spencer lived. Spencer said that he had this idea when he saw a girl bringing a wreath of flowers to the grave of her dead friend and thought how wonderful it would be if her dead companion could read the message on the card and respond to it.

It is hard to come to terms with the death of a child.

Being angry with God – how do Christians cope with tragedy?

❝ When we have reasoned as best we can how tragedies happen, how precarious life may be, how the innocent suffer, we are still not satisfied. Reason alone cannot answer our cries when those we love have been torn from us. ❞

(Robert Runcie, former Archbishop of Canterbury).

One of the hardest things for people to come to terms with is the death of a child or young person. For Christians this can be a real test of their faith. They may ask 'how can a good and loving God allow this to happen?' The writer Susan Hill describes how she felt after the death of her baby Imogen, how it challenged her Christian faith and how the funeral helped her:

❝…Imogen's death started me questioning every aspect of my once apparently sure and certain Christian belief… I questioned the existence of God, the point of life and of death, the nature of suffering and the role and relevance of the church… I had never realised before how important it is to go to funerals, not for the sake of the dead but for the comfort of the living… The vicar spoke… saying what we all felt, that he did not pretend to understand Imogen's life and death, or to have any answers, that it was a fact, that he simply had to believe that sense could be made of it sometime, somehow. ❞

(edited from *Family*, Susan Hill, 1989, Michael Joseph)

> Do not stand at my grave and weep
> I am not here, I do not sleep,
> I am a thousand winds that blow.
> I am diamond glints on snow.
> I am the sunlight on ripened grain.
> I am the gentle autumn rain.
> When you awaken in the morning's hush,
> I am the swift uplifting rush
> Of quiet birds in circled flight.
> I am the soft stars that shine at night.
> Do not stand at my grave and cry,
> I am not there; I did not die.

 **ACTIVITIES**

AO1+AO2 skills

Explain why, although she is a Christian, Susan Hill felt angry with God after Imogen's death. Why do you think the vicar wasn't able to provide an answer to the question of why a baby dies? How did the funeral help Susan?

AO2 skills **ACTIVITIES**

This poem (left) is often read at funerals. In what sense does the poem suggest the writer has not died but lives on? What comfort could you offer to someone who was recently bereaved?

The nurture of the young and the role of the family

The nurture of the young

Although families vary in how they are made up, most children are brought up in families and that is how they learn how to live with others and develop their values for living in society.

What do Christians believe about family life?

Jesus was part of a family and is described as having brothers. His mother, Mary, has a special place in Christian teaching and is treated with great reverence by Christians in many parts of the world. Jesus taught about a view of the family that challenged the traditional family structure and included those who do the will of God, a new idea of what the 'Christian family' might look like.

Christians regard the family as having an essential part to play in establishing traditional Christian values in society. However, family structures and ways of life are changing and the traditional family where children are brought up by a mother and father is no longer the norm for many people. Many Christians feel that Christianity should adapt to meet changing needs and ways of life.

Why is family life important to Christians?

Christians believe the family is important because it was created by God. Both the Old and New Testaments in the Bible teach that children should respect their parents.

St Paul wrote a letter to the newly formed church in Ephesus telling them how Christian children and parents should treat each other (see Ephesians 6:1–4).

Parents are expected to provide a good example for their children of how to live a Christian life. They may believe that they have a responsibility to have their children baptised or dedicated when they are young, to encourage them to go to church and to be confirmed or baptised when they are old enough. Children are expected to respect their parents and to care for them as they grow older.

> **Matthew 12:46–50**
>
> *While Jesus was still speaking to the crowd, his mother and brothers stood outside, wanting to speak to him. Someone told him, 'Your mother and brothers are standing outside, wanting to speak to you.' He replied to him, 'Who is my mother, and who are my brothers?' Pointing to his disciples, he said, 'Here are my mother and my brothers! For whoever does the will of my Father in heaven is my brother and sister and mother.'*

> **Exodus 20:12**
>
> *Honour your father and your mother, so that you may live long in the land the Lord your God is giving you.*

> **Ephesians 6:1–4**
>
> *Children, obey your parents in the Lord, for this is right. 'Honour your father and mother' – which is the first commandment with a promise – 'that it may go well with you and that you may enjoy long life on the earth.' Fathers, do not exasperate your children; instead, bring them up in the training and instruction of the Lord.*

How do churches try to support family life?

Churches support family life in a number of different ways:

- Most churches have baptism or **dedication** services when the members of the church promise to pray for and support the parents in bringing up their children as Christians.

- Family services are held in many churches to encourage parents to bring their children to church.

- Sunday Schools are run by many churches to teach children about Christianity and help them to live by Christian values.

- Vicars, priests and ministers run baptism and **confirmation** classes to prepare parents, **godparents** and young people to make a commitment to live a Christian life.

- Churches provide opportunities for children and young people to socialise through Youth Clubs and uniformed organisations such as the Boys' Brigade.

- Churches are involved in the running of church schools and run charities to support children and families, for example The Children's Society and the Catholic Marriage Advisory Council.

- Many churches run homes for elderly people.

ACTIVITIES

Do you have to be a Christian to bring children up to understand right and wrong? Give examples of how Christian teachings might help people to solve problems in their family life.

GradeStudio

AO2

Christian parents should bring their children up to be Christians. **[12 marks]**

The response to this statement must refer to different points of view with justification. The response will be marked by levels and the highest level will be awarded for a balanced response with your own view, supported by evidence and argument. There are four levels for AO2 responses so, let's look at the way you could structure a response to reach Level 4.

Level 1
Unpack the question so the examiner knows you have understood the issue. The key word is *should*. You need to think about reasons for and against parents bringing their children up in the faith. A first point could be that the parent promised to do this when the child was baptised.

Level 2
Go on to develop this reason with knowledge of the promises made at baptism and explain how this means that parents have a duty to bring their children up as Christians. Give another view in support of this, for example that if the parents are Christians their children will naturally be involved in their Christian lifestyle.

Level 3
Consider a different view, for example that children should not be forced against their will into any religious activities. Evaluate this view by showing that children are not able to make up their minds until they are older and parents have a right to expect their children to live according to the lifestyle of the family. Give your own view.

Level 4
Comment on the views expressed so far and then explain your own, which might be that Christian parents have the duty to bring their children up in the faith, but that when they are old enough children should be given the opportunity to make up their own minds. Remember, even though this is a Christian topic and you ought to do this automatically, you must make reference to Christianity in your response.

Christian teaching about charity and concern for others

The next two pages will help you to:

- explore why Christians believe they have a responsibility to help and care for others
- examine the work of Christian charities in caring for the poor and needy
- reflect on your own views about world poverty, the reasons for it and possible solutions.

'I tell you the truth, whatever you did for one of the least of these brothers of mine, you did for me' (Matthew 25:40b).

Charity and concern

Christianity teaches that everyone who loves God has a responsibility to care for the poor. This includes everyone, whether they are living in the next street or a distant country. Jesus set an example of helping the poor, sick, needy and outcasts of society. He used parables to teach people how they should treat others. One of his most important teachings is in the parable of the Sheep and the Goats (Matthew 25:31–46) where, at the Last Judgement, people are judged according to whether they helped those in need or not. Those who helped the poor will be chosen for Heaven.

Jesus gives examples of who the needy are and how they can be helped:
- the hungry are fed
- the thirsty are given water
- strangers are welcomed
- the naked are clothed
- the sick are cared for
- people in prison are visited.

Jesus goes on to identify himself with the poor and needy, saying that in helping them people have helped him: 'I tell you the truth, whatever you did for one of the least of these brothers of mine, you did for me.' (Matthew 25:40).

The parable of the Good Samaritan tells Christians 'Love the Lord your God with all your heart, and with all your soul, and with all your strength, and with all your mind'; and 'Love your neighbour as yourself' (Luke 10:27), which means helping your neighbour even if they are your enemy.

For Christians the two aspects (loving God and loving others) are intrinsically linked. Being kind to others without loving God, or loving God without that impacting on how someone treats others is hypocritical or, in the words of Jesus, 'whitewashed tombs' (Matthew 23:27), meaning clean on the outside but not on the inside.

In his Sermon on the Mount, Jesus says the same thing but in the opposite way. 'In everything, do to others as you would have them do to you' (Matthew 7:12). This is often referred to as the Golden Rule. Many religions and religious teachers have taught versions of this same code of conduct.

How do Christians give to charity?

Many Christians feel that they can put the teaching of Jesus that they should help and care for the poor into practice by giving to charities. Christians often choose to support a **charity** that has a Christian background. They may give a set amount of their income to charity or, if this is difficult for them, they may get involved in fund raising activities themselves. They may look at their own lifestyle and try to live ethically, supporting initiatives such as Traidcraft.

Church-related aid organisations

There are many Christian charities that work among poor and needy people all over the world. Here are three examples:

CAFOD

The Catholic Association for Overseas Development (CAFOD) and the Irish equivalent, Trócaire, work together to alleviate poverty through 500 different projects in 75 countries. CAFOD tries to tackle the causes of poverty as well as the symptoms.

Tearfund

Tearfund is committed to Christian action for the world's poor. One of their projects is to get people to think about the impact of what they buy on the people who produce the goods. This campaign is called 'Lift the Label' and aims to raise awareness of the poor pay and conditions of the workers who produce the bargain clothes we buy in high street stores.

Christian Aid: founded on faith and hope

Christians of all denominations support the work of Christian Aid whose motto is life before death. The Director of Christian Aid, Daleep Mukarji, describes its aims as:

Christian Aid is founded on the Christian Faith and based on hope. It is driven by the Gospel of good news to the poor and inspired by the vision of a new Earth where everyone lives in justice, peace and plenty.

Grade Studio

AO1

QUESTION
Explain why Christians might support a Christian aid agency. **[6 marks]**

To reach the highest levels in your response you will need to use your knowledge of an agency and explain how its work, and the reasons the organisation gives for its work, match Christian beliefs. Let's now look at what you need to do to achieve the higher level.

Level 1
Select an agency. There are three given in the specification and you should have studied one in depth. At this level the response will outline what the agency does and why, for example, Christian Aid aims to provide emergency aid, short-term aid, long-term aid and education, because it follows the teaching of Jesus, to help less fortunate people.

Level 2
Go on to explain Christian teaching about charity and concern for others. Refer for example to Jesus' actions in healing the sick and his parables such as 'the sheep and the goats' or the commandment 'love your neighbour as yourself'. Say why this relates to Christian Aid.

Level 3
Link the work of Christian Aid directly to this teaching and use any further information about the organisation to support this: for example, that Christian Aid will help all people and not just Christians, and that it aims to make people self-sufficient and give them dignity. Conclude with a brief summary of how the organisation's purpose and principles match Christian attitudes and that Christians might support it by giving money, working for the organisation or purchasing its products.

RESEARCH NOTE

Find out more about the work of the organisations CAFOD, Tearfund and Christian Aid by visiting their websites.

Religious communities

The next two pages will help you to:

- understand the role of Christian religious communities to their members and to the wider Christian community

- explore different Christian communities and describe their work

- reflect on the nature of Christian communities and their relevance to life today.

Blessed Mother Teresa caring for needy children.

What were the first Christian communities like?

Coming together in communities to share their faith has always been important for Christians. During their history Christian communities have often had to meet in secret because they were forbidden to practise their faith. The teaching of Jesus that people should love God and love their neighbour is the basis for the life of all Christian communities. The early church, which began in Jerusalem after the death and resurrection of Jesus, is described as a caring community based on the ideals of equality, sharing their possessions and eating together. They tried to implement the teaching of Jesus in practical ways.

Acts 2:42–47

They devoted themselves to the apostles' teaching and to the fellowship, to the breaking of bread and to prayer. Everyone was filled with awe, and many wonders and miraculous signs were done by the apostles. All the believers were together and had everything in common. Selling their possessions and goods, they gave to anyone as he had need. Every day they continued to meet together in the temple courts. They broke bread in their homes and ate together with glad and sincere hearts, praising God and enjoying the favour of all the people. And the Lord added to their number daily those who were were being saved.

What is a religious community?

There are groups of Christians today who try to practise this way of living. They believe that prayer is very powerful and base their lives around prayer, silent reflection and contemplation. Some Christians feel they have a vocation or calling from God to join a religious community or holy order. They choose to spend their lives praying, living and working in purity, away from the world. They may join monasteries, convents or other communities.

Religious orders are communities of men or women, mostly Roman Catholics, but also Orthodox Christians or Anglicans (Church of England), who have chosen to live according to vows of obedience, chastity and poverty. They are called monks or nuns. Most Protestants do not have religious orders.

Most religious communities devote themselves to a particular kind of vocation, for example, teaching, nursing or social work and, although they live together in a community, work with people in need in the outside world.

Life in a religious community

People are often surprised to discover that monks and nuns are real people, living and working in the 21st century. There are at least four (and often seven) times of prayer which form the pattern for the day. Every day begins and ends with prayer. Monks and nuns also witness to God through activities such as teaching, running parishes, organising retreats, creating beautiful objects like stained glass and ceramics, and inspiring others through uplifting music and worship.

Mother Teresa and the Missionaries of Charity

Mother Teresa is probably the most famous nun in recent history. When she was only 12 she felt that she had been called to give her life to God. After working in a school in Calcutta and seeing the poverty and suffering of the poorest people she founded the Missionaries of Charity, a mixed order of sisters, brothers and priests dedicated to serving the poorest of the poor.

The missionaries never try to convert people, although they may instruct them in the Christian faith if they request it. They see their job as being to help anyone in need, regardless of their race or religion.

MUST THINK ABOUT!

What jobs might be considered to be vocations? Is a vocation different from other jobs or can any job be a vocation? What difference might it make to the way someone did a job if they thought of it as a vocation?

RESEARCH NOTE

Find out more about the life of a modern monk and discuss this with others in your class.

ACTIVITIES

'Religious communities are out of date in the modern world.' Do you agree or disagree with this statement? Give reasons, drawing on examples of religious communities you have studied. Write a diary entry for a monk or a nun describing a typical day, showing how the times of prayer provide a framework for the work and creative activities.

Welcome to the Grade Studio

This topic is about how the lives of Christians are affected by their faith. The most common problem with responses to questions on these topics is that they don't refer sufficiently to Christianity. It is not that these responses are wrong but to get to the highest levels you need to show you have plenty of knowledge and understanding of the Christian teaching and attitudes that lie behind the activities of Christian individuals and communities, which you can apply as required.

Graded examples for this topic

AO1

Question

Why is the Baptism of a baby important for a Christian family?   **[6 marks]**

A **first response** might be: Baptism is a welcoming ceremony for the baby and that is why it is important.

It is true that infant baptism is a welcoming ceremony but it is much more than that, so this would be a **weak response and only achieve Level 1**.

A **good response at Level 2** would include what the first response says, would then go on to say how baptism is important because of specific reasons to do with Christian beliefs. It would also explain how the baptism welcomes the child into the family of the Church, gives the child a name and will start them on their Christian life. Finally, it would also explain that some Christians believe baptism removes original sin.

Question

Why might Christians support a Christian aid agency?   **[6 marks]**

A **first response** might be: *Everyone should help each other because you would not like to be in a situation of poverty yourself. God said 'Love your neighbour' in the Ten Commandments.*

This makes a good point with some support and it is a start. For Christians there are much more specific reasons which can be supported by the words of Jesus, other examples from the Bible and the teaching of the Church.

A **better response** at Level 2 would be: *Jesus set an example, in his life of helping the poor, sick, needy and outcast. He taught about it in the parable of the Sheep and the Goats where those who helped the poor were chosen for heaven. The parable of the Good Samaritan tells Christians to help their neighbour even if they are their enemy.*

If the response went on to refer to the reasons given by the aid agency that would help to raise it to a **good** response, achieving Level 3.

In this topic the stimulus statement for AO2 might focus on contrasting the behaviour of Christians and non-Christians. For example:

Question

'Only regular churchgoers should be allowed to marry in church.'　　　　　　　　　　**[12 marks]**

Here's how we might build a response:

Level 1
Start by showing the examiner that you understand the main issue in the question, for example you could say that marriage in church is a religious event and requires couples to make certain promises before God.

Level 2
Go on to identify an attitude to the issue, based on religious arguments, for example you could point out that some people believe only those who regularly attend church have the right to make promises before God. In this view, people who only attend church to get married are being hypocritical, in that they are making promises to a God that they may not believe in.

Level 3
Now identify an alternative point of view, and try to offer more depth to the debate. You could point out that many people have faith in God, even though they don't attend church regularly, and that such people should still be allowed to marry in church. You could also add that the act of marriage in church may help couples to start worshipping in church more regularly. Give your own view.

Level 4
Conclude with your view, supported by evidence. There are no right or wrong answers, simply make sure you support your own conclusion, for example you might conclude that marriage in church offers all couples a way to connect with the Christian faith, whether they have been regular churchgoers or not. Finish by saying that following the example of Jesus Christ, who was always open to sinners and outcasts, so the church should be always open, even to those who have not previously supported it.

These specimen answers provide an outline of how you could construct your response. Space does not allow us to give a full response. The examiner will be looking for more detail in your actual exam responses.

Remember and Reflect

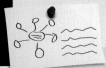

AO1 Describe, explain and analyse, using knowledge and understanding

Find the answer on:

1 Write a short definition for each of the following key words:
   a baptism   b dedication   c confirmation

PAGE 107

2 Explain the responsibilities of godparents.

PAGE 108

3 Why do Christians think marriage is important?

PAGE 112

4 What is the purpose of funerals?

PAGE 114

5 Explain what Christians believe happens after death. Which key passages from the Bible and credal statements support this belief?

PAGE 116

6 Give two reasons why Christians believe the family is very important. Support your answer with quotes from the Old and New Testaments.

PAGE 118

7 Give four examples of ways some churches try to support family life.

PAGE 119

8 Name two famous Christians who have devoted their lives to caring for others.

PAGE 122

9 What is a parable? Which two parables of Jesus give clear guidance for Christians on how they should care for others?

PAGE 120, 121

10 List the six examples which Jesus gave to show people how they should care for others.

PAGE 120

11 What is 'The Golden Rule' and how does it affect how Christians behave?

PAGE 121

12 Name two Christian organisations set up to help poor and needy people.

PAGE 121

13 Give a short, clear definition of these key words:
   a Nonconformist   b confirmation

PAGE 107

14 Give examples of two different types of Christian communities.

PAGE 123

AO2 Use evidence and reasoned argument to express and evaluate personal responses, informed insights, and differing viewpoints

Answer these questions giving as much detail as possible. You should give at least three reasons to support your response. You should also show that you have taken account of opposite opinions.

1 'The responsibilities of being a godparent should not be undertaken lightly.' Do you agree or disagree? Give reasons supporting your argument with explanations of what is involved in being a godparent.

2 'Marriage is out of date in today's world.' Do you agree or disagree? Why? How would a Christian respond to this statement?

3 'Christians have no need to be afraid of death.' What might lead someone to make this statement?

4 'The family that prays together stays together.' How does this statement support the Christian view of the family?

5 'In each suffering person you can see Jesus' (Mother Teresa). What teachings of Jesus can you link with Mother Teresa's statement? Describe how some Christians and Christian organisations have put these teachings into practice.

6 What did Jesus mean when he said 'For where two or three come together in my name, there I am with them' (Matthew 18:20). How has this been put into practice in some religious communities you have studied?

There are many Christian charities.

Topic 6: Sacred writings

The Big Picture

In this Topic you will:

- consider the importance of the Bible in the development of Christian belief
- explore how the Bible influences Christian morality and ways in which their beliefs affect the life and outlook of Christians in the world today
- express views about the importance of sacred writings and how this relates to your own experience.

What?

You will:

- develop your knowledge and understanding of key Christian beliefs about the Bible and its importance
- explain what these beliefs and ideas about the Bible mean to Christians and think about how they might affect how they live
- make links between these beliefs and ideas and what you think/believe.

Why?

Because:

- these beliefs and ideas about the Bible underpin and are reflected in the ways Christians live their lives, for example, in helping them to decide what principles they live their lives by
- understanding people's beliefs can help you understand why they think and act the way they do
- understanding these beliefs helps you compare and contrast what others believe, including thinking about your own beliefs and ideas.

How?

By:

- recalling and selecting information about Christian beliefs and ideas about the Bible, explaining its importance for people today
- thinking about the relevance of these beliefs in 21st-century Britain
- evaluating your own views about these beliefs.

Book of Kells.

GET STARTED

'The Bible is irrelevant to the world today.' Do you agree or disagree? Give reasons. Do a survey to find out what people think about this question and why.

Sacred writings

- Many of the world's great religions have a book, or books, which they consider to be sacred writings.

- A sacred book may contain the history of the religion, including the life of the founder and other key figures, and the main beliefs and teachings about how people should live. In Christianity, the sacred book is the Bible.

- The Bible contains different kinds of literature including history, laws, prophecy, poetry, the Gospels (accounts of Jesus' life and teachings), letters, the book of Acts (telling the story of the early Church), Revelation – a book written to encourage Christians under persecution.

- The Bible is made up of 66 books and is divided into two parts. The first part is the Old Testament which is made up of 39 books written before the time of Jesus. The second part is the New Testament, made up of 27 books which were written after the life of Jesus and before the end of the 2nd century CE.

- Some versions of the Bible, particularly those used by Roman Catholics, also include some books from another collection of sacred writings known as the Apocrypha.

- The Bible is important to Christians because it is a source of Christian beliefs, is a guide to life and contains the word of God.

- Many Christians believe it is the inspired word of God and is literally true.

- The Bible is used by Christians in their public and private worship.

KEY QUESTIONS

KNOWLEDGE AND UNDERSTANDING
How was the Bible compiled?

What does it contain?

Why is it important to Christians?

How do Christians use the Bible?

ANALYSIS AND EVALUATION
How can a collection of books, many written over 2000 years ago, be important today?

What do Christians mean when they say the Bible is the word of God?

How can some of the things in the Bible be true when they contradict science?

Why do different groups of Christians treat the Bible differently?

Why don't all Christians believe the same things if they all use the same book?

Apocrypha This word means hidden and is used for some of the many books that are not accepted by all Christians as being genuine parts of the scriptures.

Bible From the Greek word 'Biblia' which means books.

epistle From the Greek word for a letter. 21 such letters or epistles, from Christian leaders to Christian Churches or individuals, are included in the New Testament.

Gospels The books which contain accounts of the teachings and activities of Jesus.

Greek The original language of the New Testament.

Hebrew The original language of much of the Old Testament.

New Testament Collection of 27 books forming the second section of the Canon of Christian Scriptures.

prophecy This is not foretelling the future so much as explaining what will be the result of human behaviour.

Old Testament That part of the Canon of Christian Scriptures which the Church shares with Judaism, comprising 39 books covering the Hebrew Canon, and in the case of certain denominations, some books of the Apocrypha.

oral tradition Stories and teachings which have been remembered and passed on by word of mouth for some time before being written down.

Protestant That part of the Church which became distinct from the Roman Catholic and Orthodox Churches when their members professed the centrality of the Bible and other beliefs and protested against certain beliefs and practices of the Roman Catholic Church. Members affirm that the Bible, under the guidance of the Holy Spirit, is the ultimate authority for Christian teaching.

testament From a Latin word meaning covenant, which means an agreement.

FOR INTEREST

The Bible was not translated into English until the 14th century CE. Until then most copies were in Latin so even the few people who could read had to be able to understand Latin if they wanted to read the Bible. However, reading the Bible was forbidden except to the priests, and the Church resisted translating the Bible for many centuries. The story of how it came to be translated is one of intrigue, torture and unpleasant deaths for those who were involved. The first official version for use in English churches was published in the time of King James I of England in 1620 and is known as the Authorised Version. Since then it has been translated into almost every language in the world and is still the bestselling book. In some countries the Bible is forbidden and Christians are still persecuted for trying to publish it.

What makes a book or writings sacred?

The next two pages will help you to:

- identify the elements that make a book sacred
- examine how sacred books are seen by believers
- evaluate whether the idea of sacredness is still relevant in a secular age.

What makes a book sacred?

Sacred is another word that means holy, coming from God and bearing the authority of the divine about it.

A book or collection of writings may be sacred to the believers of a faith for several possible reasons. It may be because of its origins. Believers might think that it is important as it was written by the founder of the faith, who may well have been given its words by God. The importance of the books chosen might grow as other important members of the faith add their ideas and experiences to the writings.

Alternatively, it may have become sacred because of its content. One reason it is seen as sacred is that it may contain the teaching of its founder or contain the important part of the life and teaching of its founder. The sacred writing may also contain a record of how the faith developed, and be a source for material used in worship.

A book may become seen as sacred as believers feel that it has authority. It is accepted and revered by believers as a source of doctrines and beliefs. It may be seen as a source of guidance to help them live a good life.

Many religions see a book as sacred as they believe that it is inspired by God. They may use the term the Word of God for their Scriptures as they believe

How are these books like the Bible?

Hebrews 4:12–13

For the word of God is living and active. Sharper than any double-edged sword, it penetrates even to dividing soul and spirit, joints and marrow; it judges the thoughts and attitudes of the heart. Nothing in all creation is hidden from God's sight. Everything is uncovered and laid bare before the eyes of him to whom we must give account.

There are a variety of translations of the Bible available.

ACTIVITIES

Write a list of books you regard as important. Try to think of at least three, then, working with a partner, try to come up with a list of five important books. Why have you chosen the books you have? How are they similar and different? Why do some books survive and remain important decades after they were written and others disappear quite quickly? Share your ideas with another couple and then present your ideas to the class so that they can then form the basis of a mind map to be put into your notes.

that God has revealed the content of the book to the people who were responsible for writing it. Some believers see this Word as coming through human perception, as contained within the book. Others believe that it is literally made up of the words of God given to the people who wrote them down, that they acted as secretaries taking dictation in effect.

Is nothing sacred?

In an age where there are many different religions in existence, all competing for attention, it seems increasingly difficult to believe that one book above all others is sacred or holy. As a large number of people are secular (non-religious) in their beliefs, the idea of having a book that is sacred is increasingly difficult to communicate to others. It has also become difficult to stress the importance of a *book* as sacred because people are becoming more used to using the Internet or other media for their information.

It means that is increasingly difficult for many people to understand the hold and influence that a book like the Bible can have over shaping the ideas and beliefs of Christians, especially on moral issues.

A02 skills ACTIVITIES

'Any book can become sacred. It is about the attitude that people have to it.' What do you think? How might a Christian react? Give reasons for your answers, showing that you have thought about it from more than one point of view. Does making sacred books available online help or hinder the development of people's understandings of a faith?

What makes the Bible important to Christians?

The next two pages will help you to:

- explain why the **Old Testament** is important to Christians
- understand what it teaches
- evaluate the effects it has on Christian behaviour.

Why the Old Testament is important to Christians

The **Bible** is a collection of books (some very short indeed) which has been complied over a long period of time – probably over a thousand years. These have come to be seen as special, as revealed by God through their writers to lead Christians and others into the truths about God. Many Christians refer to the Bible as 'the Word of God'.

The first part of the Bible contains writings collected and also considered to be sacred by Jews. As Christianity began as a part of the Jewish faith and gradually developed its own organisation, these books were used by the first Christians who had been used to reading them as their Scriptures. For many Christians, these developed added importance as they began to believe that they contained prophecies about Jesus. One such passage is from the book of Isaiah, written at least 500 years before Christ.

As the Christian church began to collect its own sacred writings such as the **Gospels**, and the Epistle, this earlier collection became known as the Old Testament.

ACTIVITIES

'Christians should ignore the Old Testament and only read the **New Testament.**' How might a Christian react to this? What do you think? Give reasons for your answers, showing that you refer to Christian beliefs.

Isaiah 53:3–4

He was despised and rejected by men,
a man of sorrows, and familiar with suffering.
Like one from whom men hide their faces
he was despised, and we esteemed him not.

Surely he took up our infirmities
and carried our sorrows,
yet we considered him stricken by God,
smitten by him, and afflicted.

What types of book are there in the Old Testament?

The Pentateuch is the first five books of the Old Testament. Some Christians refer to these as the Five Books of Moses as they believe that he wrote them. These books contain accounts of the origin of the world, human beings and why the relationship between humanity and God has been broken.

The stories of the Garden of Eden, of Noah's Ark and the Tower of Babel are contained in Genesis. The book then charts the lives of Abraham, Isaac, Jacob and Joseph. In the remaining four books (Exodus to Deuteronomy), the story of the escape of the Jews from slavery in Egypt under the leadership of Moses is told. These books also tell of the giving of the Ten Commandments and the way in which God made a covenant relationship with the Jews.

ACTIVITIES

'The Ten Commandments are irrelevant to the modern world we live in.' Read them in Exodus 20. How far do you agree with the comment? Give reasons for your answer and make sure that you give a comment on each of the Ten Commandments.

The Historical Books that follow tell the story of the settlement of the promised land of Israel. These include books like Joshua, Judges, the Books of Samuel, Kings and Chronicles. They explain how Israel went from having occasional leaders called judges to developing a monarchy under kings such as Saul, David and Solomon. They contain some very honest accounts of the people involved and how they often failed to live up to God's standards. One of these is the story of David and Bathsheba, which features adultery, drunkenness, conspiracy, murder and the death of a child.

The Wisdom and Poetical Books are collections of very different types of literature. There are the prayers and hymns of the book of Psalms, which were used in worship in the Temple. There are selections of wise sayings in the Book of Proverbs. There is even an extended set of love poems in the Song of Songs.

The Prophetical Books (such as Isaiah, Ezekiel and Daniel) are records of the spokespeople God chose to speak to the nation. The Prophets challenged things they believed God was telling them were wrong as well as looking forward to a better world.

There are 15 books which are called the **Apocrypha**. People could not agree whether they should be part of the Old Testament or not and so they were collected separately. They were probably written between 200 BCE and 100 CE. Some are history and others poetry.

Some of these are printed in Roman Catholic Bibles: Tobit, Judith, the rest of Esther (Esther 10:4–10), the Epistle of Jeremiah, Ecclesiasticus, Baruch, 1 and 2 Maccabees, The History of Susanna (Daniel 13), the Song of the Three Youths, Prayer of Manasseh, Wisdom of Solomon, and Bel and the Dragon (Daniel 14).

In addition, there are more than a hundred books which form the New Testament Apocrypha. These include many more gospels, Acts of various disciples and many epistles. Some of these books are generally accepted by the Christian church even though they are not in the Bible itself:

- 1 and 2 Clement
- Shepherd of Hermas
- Didache
- Epistle of Barnabas
- Apocalypse of Peter
- The Protevangelium of James
- Third Epistle to the Corinthians.

 Grade Studio

AO1

QUESTION

State one part of the Bible. **[1 mark]**

Get used to 'state' as the flag for a factual response. There are three possible answers to this question: Old Testament; New Testament; or Apocrypha.

QUESTION

State two kinds of literature found in the Bible. **[2 marks]**

Choose two kinds of literature you could write about in more detail if you needed to, in a later part of the question. The 6-mark AO1 question or the 12-mark AO2 question could depend on what you choose in this part. Two good examples as an answer would be poetry and history.

QUESTION

Give three reasons why Christians say the Bible is important. **[3 marks]**

Notice the use of 'give' instead of state. It is just another flag word for a factual response. Possible reasons include:

1 The Bible tells us about people who have been close to God such as the Prophets.

2 The Bible tells the story of the life of Jesus.

3 It is the word of God.

Why is the New Testament important to Christians?

The next two pages will help you to:

- identify the different types of literature that make up the **New Testament**
- examine how the New Testament shapes Christian belief and action.

The Gospels

The **Gospels** are a unique form of literature. They tell the story of Jesus as well as his teachings. Two of them, Matthew and Luke, have detailed accounts of his birth. They are not biographies, as they were written for the purpose of showing how Jesus was the Son of God. They do not tell us about large parts of his life but give us extraordinary detail about the last week of his life. Three of the Gospels, Matthew, Mark and Luke, share material in common and are referred to as the Synoptic (which means 'seen together') Gospels.

ACTIVITIES

'The Gospels can tell us only limited amounts about the life of Jesus.' What do you think? How might a Christian reply? Give reasons for your answers, showing that you have referred to Christian belief.

> **Mark 15:21–24**
>
> *A certain man from Cyrene, Simon, the father of Alexander and Rufus, was passing by on his way in from the country, and they forced him to carry the cross. They brought Jesus to the place called Golgotha (which means The Place of the Skull). Then they offered him wine mixed with myrrh, but he did not take it. And they crucified him. Dividing up his clothes, they cast lots to see what each would get.*

The Acts of the Apostles

This book is an account of the beginning of the Christian church after the ascension of Jesus and particularly of the work of St Peter and St Paul in establishing churches across the Roman world.

> **Acts 2:1–4**
>
> *When the day of Pentecost came, they were all together in one place. Suddenly a sound like the blowing of a violent wind came from heaven and filled the whole house where they were sitting. They saw what seemed to be tongues of fire that separated and came to rest on each of them. All of them were filled with the Holy Spirit and began to speak in other tongues as the Spirit enabled them.*

The Epistles

These are letters from the first leaders of the faith to other Christians. Some of these were written before the Gospels and contain advice to the Christians about lifestyle. They contain the beginning of Christian theology. The Epistles have passages that are used in church services today. This extract is often used in weddings.

> **1 Corinthians 13:4–8a**
>
> *Love is patient, love is kind. It does not envy, it does not boast, it is not proud. It is not rude, it is not self-seeking, it is not easily angered, and it keeps no record of wrongs. Love does not delight in evil but rejoices with the truth. It always protects, always trusts, always hopes, and always perseveres. Love never fails.*

The Book of Revelation

Revelation, the last book of the New Testament, tries to encourage Christians who were suffering persecution from the Roman Empire. It is known as the book of Revelation of John and is written in a style which suggests it is telling people about the end of the world when evil will be defeated and justice will prevail.

> **Revelation 21:1–4**
>
> *Then I saw a new heaven and a new earth, for the first heaven and the first earth had passed away, and there was no longer any sea. I saw the Holy City, the New Jerusalem, coming down out of heaven from God, prepared as a bride beautifully dressed for her husband. And I heard a loud voice from the throne saying, 'Now the dwelling of God is with men, and he will live with them. They will be his people, and God himself will be with them and be their God. He will wipe every tear from their eyes. There will be no more death or mourning or crying or pain, for the old order of things has passed away.'*

AO2 skills ACTIVITIES

The book of Revelation has a picture of a new heaven and a new earth to describe how a perfect society might look. What do you think needs to happen for there to be a more perfect society?

GradeStudio

AO1

QUESTION

Explain why the Gospels are important to Christians.

[6 marks]

There are three levels for AO1 but this does not mean there are 2 marks per level. Examiners are looking for depth of understanding, which might be shown by referring to several different reasons briefly or by explaining two reasons fully. You could build a good response in this way:

Level 1

Begin with the most obvious point that the Gospels contain information about Jesus and so are significant for Christians because he is the founder of the faith.

Level 2

Develop this either by referring to another reason, such as the belief that the Gospels were written by people who had first-hand experience of Jesus and are therefore reliable, or by expanding the first point by describing the kind of information about Jesus that they contain and explaining why this is important. For example, they show Jesus to be the Saviour by his actions and his death and resurrection.

Level 3

Expand this with reference other important contents of the Gospels such as Jesus' moral teaching in the Sermon on the Mount. Then draw the aspects of the response together with a comment about how, because of these contents, the Gospels are crucial to keep Christians in touch with what the first Christians believed.

How the Bible is used by Christians in worship

> **The next two pages will help you to:**
>
> - explain how the **Bible** is used in public worship
> - examine how the Bible has helped shape public Christian worship
> - evaluate the importance of the Bible for worship.

How can you find a reference in the Bible?

To make it easier to use, each book of the Bible was divided into chapters and then smaller pieces of text known as verses. This is usually written like this: Luke 10:8 which means Luke's Gospel chapter 10 verse 8.

The Bible in public worship

The Bible is used by Christians in many ways: in public worship in churches or chapels – it has a central importance. It has helped to shape the ceremonies and services of the faith.

During Sunday services, there are readings from the Bible. In the Church of England, there is often a reading from both the Old and the New Testament in all services. They follow a lectionary, which is a book which orders the readings chosen from the Bible by themes and is often designed to cover the whole Bible across three years.

Alternatively, readings might be chosen that are appropriate to a particular festival, for example readings during a carol service will be about or linked to the themes of the birth of Jesus. Many churches use a set of Biblical passages in which the story of Christmas is put in the context of **Old Testament prophecy** as well as the Nativity stories themselves. This is known as the service of nine lessons and carols.

A stained glass picture of the Crucifixion.

The Bible and Christian worship

For many centuries, the Bible was not available in printed form and churches might only have one copy which the priest or minister might read from. Until the time of the Reformation, these were often written in Latin. The practice of putting stained glass windows into churches developed to help those who could not read or understand Latin to become familiar with the Biblical stories by seeing them represented in pictures.

It is common to find in many churches a copy of the Ten Commandments hung up in a prominent place to make sure the congregation knew what they were. As these were for many centuries the basis of the laws of the country, there was both a spiritual and political reason for doing this.

The Bible reading or a verse from the passages read in church can become the basis of the talk or sermon that the priest or minister gives to the congregation. For many churches, the sermon is an important moment as it emphasises the importance of Scripture in the Christian life.

The Bible has become the source or basis of many prayers. The most famous of these is the Lord's Prayer. This is based on a prayer that Jesus taught his disciples (see Topic 4.9).

Other Biblical prayers such as the Magnificat (Mary's song in Luke Chapter 1) or the Nunc Dimittis (from Luke 2) have become the basis of prayers regularly used. The Psalms have often been used as prayer or to inspire it in services. There many other parts of the Bible that may be drawn upon.

ACTIVITIES

'In order to be true to the faith of Jesus, the Bible has to be at the centre of Christian worship.' What do you think? Give reasons, using evidence from this chapter and your own knowledge to justify your answer. What problems might a church encounter trying to use the Bible to aid its worship today?

As many parts of the Bible are poetry they can easily be set to music – especially the Psalms. Hymns will either directly or indirectly draw upon a part of the Bible to help worship God. One of the most well known of these is 'The Lord's my shepherd', which is a version of the twenty-third Psalm and is often sung at funerals.

Sections from the story of the Last Supper form the most important words of the Eucharist. The giving of the bread and wine by Jesus and his description of them as his body and blood are often explained by either reading from one of the **Gospels** or using a passage that the apostle Paul wrote in his letter 1 Corinthians.

How the Bible is used in private worship

The next two pages will help you to:

- explain how the **Bible** is used in private worship
- examine how the Bible has helped Christians in their lives
- demonstrate the way the Bible affects a Christian's decisions.

The Bible and private worship

Many Christians believe that they need regularly to read the Bible in private. They may well study a part of it each day as part of a private time of prayer and reflection at the beginning or the end of the day. These portions of the Bible may be read each day as a source of inspiration to find the strength to face the world. Such Christians believe that this will help to support the believer before going out into the world. Evangelical Christians have referred to this as their 'Quiet Time', when they are quiet before God in order to think about how they can face the challenges of the day.

A reading from the Bible may be used as a basis for meditation. Christians may take a story from the Bible and try to imagine themselves as being there in order to try to think about its meaning for them today. For example the story of the stilling of the storm by Jesus can help them deal with difficult times.

ACTIVITIES

Read the story of the stilling of the storm in Mark 4:35–41. Shut your eyes and try to run through the story in your mind and then try to write down your feelings about what happens. How might this story help a Christian who is going through a difficult time? What sort of storms might a person face during their lives? Draw a mind map to show some of them.

'Christ orders the storm to cease' by Wilhelm Kretzschmer, 1884 (Luke 8:22–25).

Many Christians read the Bible privately as a source of comfort and guidance.

A reading from the Bible may be used as a basis for prayer, with Christians taking the ideas of the portion and trying to apply it to one's own life. The believer may use a schedule and some explanatory notes to assist with this daily reading. One of the organisations that produces different types of notes and aids to do this is Scripture Union. These are produced normally three or four times a year.

One Christian who has encouraged Christians to read the Bible daily (if possible) is the Church of England minister and international speaker John Stott. He has called the Bible a kind of love letter which enables the Christian to understand Christ. It is not to be seen as something from the past, but something vital to help live today.

John Stott has said that Christians need to be double-listeners – to the Bible and to the culture they live in – in order to communicate the Christian message.

Many Christians are encouraged regularly to memorise verses of the Bible to help with the questions of others and to help them develop their own understanding of faith. These may also help to support the believer during the day.

A book of comfort

The Bible may be used as a source of comfort, providing words that can help a person deal with a difficult situation, for example some Christians might find these quotations from Isaiah encouraging.

 **ACTIVITIES**

Using the Internet, research the work of the Bible Society or Scripture Union and produce a PowerPoint presentation or a mini-project about how these organisations try to help people read the Bible today.

'The Bible is essentially a handbook of salvation' (John Stott). What do you think this means? What else do you think Christians would want to say about the importance of the Bible?

Isaiah 40:29–31
*He gives strength to the weary
and increases the power of the weak.
Even youths grow tired and weary,
and young men stumble and fall;
but those who hope in the Lord
will renew their strength.
They will soar on wings like eagles;
they will run and not grow weary,
they will walk and not be faint.*

How does the Bible help to develop Christian belief?

The next two pages will help you to:

- explain how the Bible has helped to shape Christian belief
- examine how it influences Christian belief and actions
- evaluate the effects it has on Christian behaviour.

 **ACTIVITIES**

What do you think influences what a person believes about the world? Write a list and then share this with a partner. Share your ideas with the rest of the class and then create a mind map to show these different ideas.

Pope Benedict XVI. He has a great influence on what Roman Catholics think and do.

The Bible as a source of belief

The **Bible**, especially the **New Testament**, is considered by **Protestant** Christians to be the source of their doctrines and beliefs as it is the word of God, or contains the word of God. The authority of Scripture is above the authority of any other person, writing or book.

Other denominations, such as Roman Catholics, consider the Bible to be a superior source of authority in matters of belief and doctrine but see other sources of authority as important as well. They have developed in line with the teaching and themes of the Bible. This includes, for example, the writings of other saints (such as St Augustine or St Thomas Aquinas), the decisions of Ecumenical Councils, and statements from the Pope such as Encyclicals on important issues.

The Bible and belief and actions

The Bible is a basis and guide for Christians for their moral and ethical conduct. The Ten Commandments are an obvious example. They give instructions about issues such as murder, adultery, honouring your father and mother, not stealing and not lying. There is debate within Christian churches as to what some of these mean in today's world. For some Christians, the commandment about not allowing murder does not just apply to murder, but they may use it to justify their views on abortion, euthanasia or war.

With the teaching of Jesus in the **Gospels** telling people that when they plan to do an action in their head that can be a sin, the commandments are now seen as not just about an act that is wrong but about having the intention to do something sinful.

Many Christians believe that the entire Bible can be used to help them develop their own social and moral thinking. Others take a more selective approach, saying that the **Old Testament** contains rules or instructions that may well not fit in the modern world, for example where in Leviticus 18:22 it says 'Do not lie with a man as one lies with a woman; that is detestable.'

Some Christians believe that this is homophobic and comes from a time when people did not understand what causes a person's sexuality. They say that although the Bible contains the Word of God, it also contains the words of human beings and that you need to study the Bible closely to see which is which. Other Christians argue that the moral teaching of the Bible is timeless and cannot be changed to reflect the modern world.

Many of Jesus' parables instruct Christians about how to treat their fellows. Many of the stories in the Bible are morally instructive. However there is no clear guidance on some moral issues such as abortion, contraception, or warfare, leading to differences of opinion amongst Christians.

RESEARCH NOTE

Research the work of Tearfund. How does it show Christian belief and morality from the Bible in action? Present your findings as a leaflet explaining their work to someone who wants to find out about what they do.

AO1+AO2 skills ACTIVITIES

'What would Jesus do?' is not a good slogan to live your life by, as Jesus lived in a much simpler age. What do you think? How might a Christian reply? Show in your answer at least two different ideas about how the Bible is seen by Christians.

Research the work of Tearfund. How does it show Christian belief and morality from the Bible in action? Present your findings as a leaflet explaining their work to someone who wants to find out about what they do.

How do Christians show respect to the Bible?

How the Bible is treated in action

The Bible is a very important book to Christians and they try to show its value to them. There are many different ways in which Christians may show their respect for the Bible in worship.

In one of the **Protestant** Churches, the Presbyterian Church, the Bible may be brought in before the service begins and set on the lectern in the pulpit which is in the centre at the front of the church. This emphasises the huge significance of the word of God. By having the pulpit in a central place in the church (instead of to one side as is generally found in Church of England and Roman Catholic churches) the importance of the Bible is reinforced.

In other Churches, such as the Church of England, the Bible is set on a special lectern which may be richly decorated. This is often in the shape of an eagle (being made from either wood or metal), as a sign that the word of God is being spread across the world. The lessons may be read or chanted either by a priest or by a member of the congregation. The lectern is normally set in the front of the church, so that the Scripture reader faces the congregation.

In some Churches, the Bible may be taken into the centre of the church by the priest to read the Gospel at the Eucharist. There may be a group of people holding candles either side of the priest while they are reading. This is a way of symbolically reminding people that Jesus said that he would be the Light of the World.

As well as being read, the Bible will be important to the sermon. Some Christians might lift the Bible by raising their hands as they begin to preach as a way to show the supremacy of the Bible as the word of God.

In some Churches, there may be an opportunity for members of the church to come to the front and share any insights they have gained from how the Bible has spoken to their lives in some way.

The next two pages will help you to:

- explain how the **Bible** is shown respect by Christians
- evaluate the different ways the Bible is treated
- explore how Christian behaviour towards the Bible reflects beliefs.

AO1 skills ACTIVITIES

Imagine that an important person like the Queen or the Prime Minister is coming to visit your school. How might the school prepare for their visit? How do these actions link to the idea about the respect the person is shown? Share your ideas with the rest of the class.

Lectern in the shape of an eagle.

Getting the words right

The Bible is a book that has been shaped by many things. The **Old Testament** was written mostly in **Hebrew** while the New Testament was written mostly in **Greek**. For centuries, churches used Latin translations of the Scriptures.

Many people such as John Wycliffe and William Tyndale in Britain and Martin Luther in Germany began to say that it was important that people were able to read the Scriptures in their own languages, rather than in foreign ones. With the invention of printing, it became possible for people to own their own copies. In the Victorian era for example, it was often seen as a necessity that there should be a family Bible which would be read as part of a family prayer time.

Many Christians became increasingly interested in what the words of the Bible were in the original languages and were keen to make sure that the words were accurately translated from the original tongue to the one they were reading it in.

There are many disputes about what passages of the Bible mean: for example some people believe that the story of the woman caught in adultery brought to Jesus in John's Gospel was not an original part of the book but was added later. In Mark's Gospel, many scholars think that we have lost the original ending of the book and that the final verses were added on at a later date.

Some Christians describe themselves as literalists or fundamentalists, that is, they say that every word of the Bible has to be literally true in order to have authority. They believe that the world was created as the book of Genesis says and that if science tries to explain it another way, then science is wrong.

All Christians believe that the Bible has authority but they differ in how far this extends and how much they should try to express or shape their views with regard to the modern world.

Painting of Martin Luther by Karl Bauer.

AO2 skills ACTIVITIES

Research the life of Martin Luther. What did he teach about the Bible and its importance to the Christian life? 'The Bible is one book amongst many.' What do you think a Christian would say to this? What do you think? Give reasons for your answers, making sure that you use Christian teaching and practice to illustrate your answer.

Is the Bible true?

Beliefs about truth and the Bible

What do we mean by true? True usually means that something which has been said is factually accurate and can be checked. If the Bible is true, must anything it says be factually correct? Not necessarily, many Christians might say.

There are amazing stories in the Bible which seem to contradict modern science, according to many people. Miracles of healing, control of natural events and the story of the creation of the world for some people are at odds with a universe that can be explained in a scientific way. Before dismissing the Bible as not being actually true think about the following.

The Bible was written before there was any scientific knowledge of the universe and space. The laws of science were unknown. Disease was sometimes considered to be punishment for wrongdoings or because the person was taken over by a demon. So, is it wrong to expect the Bible to contain scientific answers to question such as when and how did the world begin?

Another way to look at it is people spend hours watching programmes, or reading books, that are fiction and so therefore untrue, but they still mean something to them. In fact they often contain very important truths. The plays of Shakespeare, even the historical ones, are often inaccurate and untrue factually, but they are very important as conveying meaning about the characters and they speak to the audience.

The Bible and myth

Ancient peoples also used story to convey meanings. Looking at the meaning behind the stories shows that the truth is personal rather than factual, poetic or even mythological. By myth these Christians mean stories told in ancient cultures which reflected their beliefs and supported them. Often they included fantastic or supernatural events.

An example would be the flood story in Genesis. Some people who worry whether it is scientifically true or not have missed the point. It is actually a story to support and teach the belief that God is generous and prefers to save people rather than to punish. Scholars have shown over the last 150 years that much of the Bible is factually true. It would be wrong to dismiss the Bible as a whole by misunderstanding it.

The next two pages will help you to:

- describe the different beliefs about truth and the **Bible** that believers have
- understand the meaning of myth in the Bible
- evaluate whether the Bible has a purpose in a modern society.

AO2 skills ACTIVITIES

'The Bible is inspired by God.' What does a person who says this mean? What other views are there among Christians about the Bible? What do you think is the most reasonable one to adopt?

Other Christians take the view that the Bible is factually true, seeing it as the actual words of God in all respects and that science is wrong or at least must be questioned. The Bible is inspired by God and is His word. Some Christians believe that it is possible to unite the Genesis story and scientific views. People who hold this view are sometimes known as Creationists and may also be literalists believing each word of the Bible to be the actual word of God.

Some Christians would take the view that this debate is just a distraction from what is really important and that it does not matter because the moral teaching comes through whether the stories are literally true or not. These Christians would say that the word of God is not identical to the words of the Bible but it comes through the Bible to the believer as he or she reads it. Christians who take this view believe that the Bible is inspiring and that God speaks to them personally guiding their conduct and gives them spiritual support regardless of whether the Bible is factually true.

 **FOR DEBATE**

'If the Bible is made up, then it cannot be used to help us to live good lives now.' How might a Christian answer this?

  GradeStudio

AO2

QUESTION

'Some parts of the Bible are so out of date they should be removed.' **[12 marks]**

Remember that for AO2 questions, responses must give different views about the issue in the question and for Level 4, you must give your own view. Views must be supported with evidence and argument. Examiners use levels of response which enable examiners to credit a wide range of responses but to ensure that you reach the highest level you need to build the response through the levels in an organised way. Let's now look at what you need to do to achieve a high level.

Level 1

Explain the significance of the issue in the statement and then offer at least one view about it. Identify a part of the Bible that could be considered out of date and use it as an example for discussion. You could select a story from the Old Testament that suggests that God is a violent God, such as the plagues experienced by the Egyptians or the slaughter of Israel's enemies by Joshua or King David. Or you could choose the story of creation in Genesis which seems to contradict modern scientific knowledge.

Level 2

Go on to develop the response by explaining the way in which the material chosen is out of date, perhaps because science has better explanations for the beginning of the world or because Christians do not believe that God would favour killing, because Jesus was peaceful.

Level 3

Offer an alternative view with justification, for example that the Bible records how people gradually began to understand that God is a loving God. The bloody history and poor understanding of the nature of God gradually gives way through the Old Testament Prophets to the God of love in the teaching of Jesus. Give your own view.

Level 4

Now express your own view and support it with evidence and argument. For example you could say that it would be wrong to remove parts of the Bible because it is all part of the rich tradition of the Church, but this does not mean all parts should be taken as equally important. So for Christians the New Testament is more important but we need the Old Testament as well to understand the novelty of Jesus' life and teaching.

Welcome to the Grade Studio

In this grade studio we will look at the longer AO1 responses required to part d of the question, which is worth 6 marks. Part d of each question will be marked according to levels. For AO1, there are three levels. A good response to part d will be well organised, contain relevant knowledge and have a full, well developed explanation. If required, you should analyse the topic which means you might make a comparison between two aspects of the topic.

Graded examples for this topic

AO1

Question

Describe two kinds of literature in the Bible and explain why they might be important to Christians. **[6 marks]**

Key words in this question are: describe, explain and important.

Student's answer

The Bible contains poetry and Gospels. Christians use the poetry which is in the Psalms for some of their hymns and sing them in their worship. They use the Gospels to tell them about the life of Jesus.

Examiner's comment

This is a start to responding to the question, but the description is weak. The explanation only refers to the literature being important because it is used in worship or for information about Jesus. There is no real explanation. This response would just scrape into Level 1.

Student's improved answer

The Bible contains poetry and Gospels. Much of the poetry is found in the book of Psalms, but there is poetry elsewhere in the Bible, for example in the books of the prophets. The Psalms were written, according to tradition, by King David and are used in worship by Christians.

The poetry is important to Christians because: the content of many poems is helpful and comforting, they are used in worship and they link Christians today to worshippers in the past. As the Bible is the word of God the Psalms tell Christians about God, what he wants from people and how he can help them. The 23rd Psalm is particularly comforting because it tells Christians that God is like a good shepherd, looking after them as they go through all the problems and difficulties of life.

The Gospels tell Christians about the life of Jesus, what he did and said. They are not a biography and have very few details about Jesus as a person. They explain why Christians believe Jesus to be the Messiah and Son of God and how he is their saviour. They are used in worship as one of the readings in a service. They are believed by some Christians to have been written by people who knew Jesus which makes them especially important.

Examiner's comment

This gives a better account of two types of literature. It is still quite vague for the poetry but better for the Gospels. The explanation of the importance of each is good because it goes beyond just saying they are used in worship and explains why that is important. The response also explains the central importance of the Gospels for Christian belief and backs that up by reference to their authorship. This is a good response and could be judged at Level 3 depending on how well it was developed in the exam. It has all the basic features of a good response.

Questions might focus on these issues:
* whether a book as ancient as the Bible can be of any value today
* whether the Bible is the most important source of authority for Christians
* whether the Bible is the most important item for a Christian to use in personal worship.

Question

The Bible is ancient so it must be out of date.   **[12 marks]**

> For AO2 Questions, to achieve Levels 3 and 4, you must refer to Christianity. You will be reminded of this in the instructions on the exam paper.

Remember that AO2 is about examining points of view and expressing your own views, using evidence and argument to support them. Examiners will use levels of response to judge the quality of your work and the best responses will have plenty of evidence to support different points of view. For AO2 there are four levels of response and for the top level the response will have a personal view supported by evidence and argument.

Plan your response carefully so it is clearly organised and tells the examiner exactly what you want.

	Content	Level
First step: Begin by telling the examiner briefly what the issues are.	It might be true to say that ancient books contain nothing which is of any use today. Although the Bible is very important for Christians it does not really help people to make up their minds about modern day issues.	**Level 1.** At this point, the response is simplistic and with limited viewpoints which are not supported with evidence or argument.
Second step: Identify different views to the issue and explain them.	It might be true to say that ancient books contain nothing which is of any use today. Although the Bible is very important for Christians it does not really help people to make up their minds about modern day issues. However, many Christians would say that the important things in the Bible are not affected by its age because they are about how humans behave and what they believe.	**Level 2.** At this point, the response shows understanding of the issues and several points of view have been identified with some support. The addition of a personal viewpoint would take this answer to Level 3.
Third step: Give a full explanation for each view. Use appropriate technical terms.	It might be true to say that ancient books contain nothing which is of any use today. Although the Bible is very important for Christians it does not really help people to make up their minds about modern day issues. However, many Christians would say that the important things in the Bible are not affected by its age because they are about how humans behave and what they believe. Some people might say that the Bible contradicts science but Christians might argue that the stories of creation were not meant to be taken literally, they just say that God is the creator. I think the Bible needs to be reinterpreted.	**Level 3.** This answer needs some more detail and support for the personal viewpoint to reach Level 4.
Fourth step: Conclude with your own view, with evidence to support it.	It might be true to say that ancient books contain nothing which is of any use today. Although the Bible is very important for Christians it does not really help people to make up their minds about modern day issues. However, many Christians would say that the important things in the Bible are not affected by its age because they are about how humans behave and what they believe. Some people might say that the Bible contradicts science but Christians might argue that the stories of creation were not meant to be taken literally, they just say that God is the creator. Personally, I think that the Bible does contain important truths but needs to be reinterpreted for use today.	**Level 4.** This is now a good answer which contains different supported viewpoints as well as a supported personal view.

These specimen answers provide an outline of how you could construct your response. Space does not allow us to give a full response. The examiner will be looking for more detail in your actual exam responses.

Remember and Reflect

AO1 Describe, explain and analyse, using knowledge and understanding

Find the answer on:

1 Explain, in one sentence, what each of the following means:
   a Old Testament   b New Testament   c Gospel

PAGE 131

2 Why is the Bible important to Christians?

PAGE 134

3 Explain what Christians understand by the term the Word of God.

PAGE 132

4 Explain what Christians mean by the authority of the Bible.

PAGE 132

5 Why do Christians believe the Old Testament is important?

PAGE 134

6 Explain, giving examples, the different types of books you will find in the Old Testament.

PAGE 135

7 Explain, giving examples, the different types of books you will find in the New Testament.

PAGE 136

8 Explain, in one sentence, what each of the following words means:
   a prophecy   b Psalms   c Gospels

PAGE 131, 134

9 Outline three ways in which Christians use the Bible in public worship.

PAGE 138

10 Outline three ways in which Christians use the Bible in private worship.

PAGE 140

11 Write a sentence to explain the following:
   a lectern   b sermon   c Eucharist

PAGE 139, 144

The Bible can help Christians in many ways.

AO2 Use evidence and reasoned argument to express and evaluate personal responses, informed insights, and differing viewpoints

1   Answer the following, giving as much detail as possible. You should give at least three reasons to support your response and also show that you have taken into account opposite opinions.
   a   Christians must find it difficult to believe in the Bible as being literally true in today's world.
   b   Do you think Christian teaching contained in the Bible is relevant in today's world?
   c   Do you believe the Bible is a holy book from God? Why or why not? Compare your response with that of an evangelical Christian, a liberal Christian and an atheist.
   d   What would you say are the essential things a Christian has to believe about the Bible? Why?

2   'The Bible is a library of books, not just one book.' How does this help Christians explain the importance of the Bible? What problems might the idea of the Bible being a library cause?

3   Draw this table out and fill it in to form the basis of an essay about the relevance of the Ten Commandments.

The Ten Commandments	I think this commandment is relevant/irrelevant because
1 You shall not worship any other God.	
2 You shall not make a graven image.	
3 You shall not take the name of God in vain (as a swear word).	
4 You shall not break the Sabbath.	
5 You shall not dishonour your parents.	
6 You shall not murder.	
7 You shall not commit adultery.	
8 You shall not steal.	
9 You shall not lie.	
10 You shall not covet what is other people's.	

Exam**Café**

Welcome

Welcome to Exam Café. Here you can get ready for your exam through a range of revision tools and exam preparation activities designed to help you get the most out of your revision time.

Tools and tips

Now you have finished the Topics, it is time to revise and prepare for the examination. Before this sends you into a panic with all those worries you have about coping in the exam situation, remember that as you have worked through the course you have gained knowledge, understanding and skills. Yes, you will have to refresh your memory and practise your skills but this section of the book is intended to help you to do those things effectively and ensure you do justice to yourself in the exam.

The key to good revision is to 'work smart'. This section will guide you to know what is needed for success and just as important, what is not. So don't panic! Think positive because the examiner will. GCSE is about what you can do, not what you can't.

Key points

1 Your revision needs to focus on what the examiners want in your answers, so you can get the best possible marks.
   a In GCSE Religious Studies there are **two things** that examiners are looking for. These are described in the assessment objectives – AO1 and AO2.
   b Each assessment objective is worth 50% of the marks.
2 You need to understand that the exam questions are designed to measure your performance in each assessment objective. This will ensure you know how respond to the questions so as to reach the highest levels. Each question will have five parts:
   a Four assessing AO1 – three questions checking on your knowledge, one measuring understanding and analysis.
   b One question assessing AO2 – assessing your ability to put different points of view on an issue, weight them up against each other and express your own views backing everything up with evidence and good arguments.
   If this all sounds rather scary don't worry. As you work though this section you will see that by knowing what examiners want in each part of the question you can make your revision really count because it will be well focused on success in the assessment objectives.

How to get started

You do need to have a sound knowledge and understanding of all you have studied, so there is some basic factual learning to be done. Techniques for revision are quite personal and depend on how you learn things best. Here are some suggestions.

- Create summary cards to summarise a unit, or a part of unit, on a small card with between 5 and 10 bullet points on it.

- Design memory cards. These are really good if you are a visual learner. Use pictures, or other visual prompts, to recall key facts or, for example, the order of events in a marriage service.

- Break your revision time up into intensive revision session of 5–10 minutes. Give yourself a break (no more than 5 minutes), then test yourself on what you have revised.

- Write your own questions. Write mark schemes for them. Answer the questions and use the levels of response to mark them.

- Set everything you learn in the context of Christianity, as a living faith practised today by 21st-century people.

- Cover all parts of each section of the course.

- Know the meaning of all the technical (religious) words in the specification. Learn a short definition for each of them, which you could explain if necessary and use them in your revision notes.

- Make connections in your revision between what you know, and how and why this is important for Christians. Use spider charts for this if that will help you to recall the connections.

Remember only 25% of the marks are awarded for knowledge. A further 25% depend on you showing an understanding of what you know. So, although knowledge revision is important it is only the basis for you being able to do well in the understanding questions for AO1 and the skills questions for AO2.

Revision
Common mistakes

Wasting valuable time
A question worth 1 mark does not need a paragraph response. Match the length of responses to the mark allocations and don't waste time.

Misreading the question
Of course this will never happen to you, but a surprising number of candidates answer a question which they think has been asked rather than the one that has actually been asked. They see a key word and miss the point of the question losing most of the marks as a result.

Poor selection of knowledge
Choose good examples which focus on the religious aspect of the topic, for example the response to the question why do Christians baptise infants? – 'because they like a good welcome party for the child' is not a good response from a religious studies point of view. 'Baptism is a way of welcoming the child into the family of the Church' is much better and will get more marks.

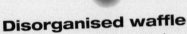

Disorganised waffle
AO2 responses in particular need to be planned, otherwise you will waffle and muddle along. In your revision, practice planning responses and then write the plan up, so you get into the habit and feel confident to do this in the exam. If you feel strongly about an issue in an A02 response, make sure you take a step back and think calmly about other points of view. A long rant about your view will get few marks.

Getting hung up on your view of an issue
This is a real danger when you feel strongly about the issue in the AO2 stimulus. You must consider various views and have balance as well as your own opinion in the answer.

Using the same information over and over again
Using the same information for different questions but in different contexts (for example, repeatedly using the parable of the Good Samaritan) may be appropriate but don't expect the examiner to credit you with many marks unless you link the comment to each of the topics. The parable of the Good Samaritan is not the only parable in the Bible. Candidates who use it over and over again to justify the beliefs or actions of Christians cannot expect to get many marks.

Revision check list

TOPIC 1 CORE BELIEFS

This section has lots of technical terms which you should use, but make sure you use them correctly and show the examiner that you really know what they mean rather than just dropping them into the answer for effect.

TOPIC 2 SPECIAL DAYS AND PILGRIMAGES

Focus your responses on the religious activities, the spiritual effects and value of the special days or place of pilgrimage. Only include more social non-religious benefits as additional material, for example – 'Pilgrimage is an opportunity to focus on doing something for your spiritual benefit.' This is much more valuable as a Religious Studies response than 'Pilgrimage gives people a break from their daily lives.'

TOPIC 3 MAJOR DIVISIONS AND INTERPRETATIONS

This can be a really confusing section. Make a table of three columns broken into sections to list similarities and differences. Try to see the connection between what the different groups believe and how they worship and organise themselves.

TOPIC 4 PLACES AND FORMS OF WORSHIP

In this unit candidates often select weak examples for the knowledge questions which makes it less easy to get high marks. Pews are a feature of many churches, but there is much less to say about them than the altar or font. Go for items that are only found in a church and that have symbolic or religious value. The vicar and the choir are NOT features of a church building.

TOPIC 5 RELIGION IN THE FAITH COMMUNITY AND THE FAMILY

Concentrate on religious aspects of the events and activities, not on the cultural or social – for example, marriage as public promises before God rather than an opportunity to wear a special dress and have a good time with friends.

TOPIC 6 SACRED WRITINGS

Actually read some of the Bible so you answer questions from first-hand knowledge. Read for example the story of Jesus' trial and execution in Mark's Gospel or the creation stories in Genesis. This will give your responses more realism and greater value.

ExamCafé

Exam preparation
Sample student answer

Now you have done some serious revision it is time to see what sort of response to the questions will get good marks in the exam. Here are some examples of responses with comments from the examiner to show you what is good about them and how they could be improved.

Remember examiners will use levels of response for part d which is AO1 and part e which is AO2. For parts a, b and c responses will be point marked. This means that if there is 1 mark allocated for the question, only one point is expected, if 2 marks are allocated, then two points are expected and so on. Part a is worth 1 mark, b 2 marks and c 3 marks.

AO1

Here are some AO1 point marked questions and example responses from Topic 1.

Topic 1 Core beliefs

Name one person of the Trinity   [1 mark]

God the Father

Examiner says
Correct: Be careful, because the response should be one of 'God the Father', 'God the Son' or 'God the Holy Spirit'.

Give two attributes of the Trinity   [2 marks]

1 All persons are equal
2 There are 3 persons

Examiner says
Response 1 is correct but response 2 does not give an attribute. A correct second response would be that all three persons are eternal.

Why is the Trinity important?   [3 marks]

1 The Trinity helps to explain how Jesus could also be God.
2 The Trinity reminds Christians that God is three persons.
3 The Trinity is a way of expressing the different experiences Christians have of God.

Examiner says
Three good reasons given.

AO2

And now to part e/AO2. This part of each question is worth 12 marks or 50% of the total. It really important that you learn how to respond to the statements in a way that will ensure you get the best marks possible by hitting the highest Level. There are four levels for AO2. Remember AO2 is about expressing views, including your own, about an issue, backing the views up with good evidence and argument.

Topic 4 Places and forms of worship

'Reading the Bible is the most important part of a Christian's religious life.' Discuss this statement. You should include different, supported points off view and a personal viewpoint. You must refer to Christianity in your answer.

[12 marks]

Response 1

The Bible is important to Christians for several reasons. It is a holy book with stories of Jesus and other people who were close to God. Christians like to read about them so it is important to their life. Other things are just as important in a Christian's religious life, such as praying.

Examiner says
This is Level 1. Two relevant viewpoints are stated but there is little support to back them up. This is a simplistic response and shows little understanding of the question. There is no use of technical terms.

Response 2

The Bible is important to Christians for several reasons, but this does not mean it is the most important part of their religious life. It is important to Christians because of what it contains such as the life and teaching of Jesus. It is also important because it is the basis of Christian beliefs and because it is the word of God. It is also a guide for how Christians should live. Other things are important to Christians such as helping the poor, prayer or celebrating the Eucharist. I think The Bible is the most important because without it, there would be no Christianity.

Examiner says
This is Level 2. The first sentence is good as it explains to the examiner what the candidate understands the question to be about. However, although several viewpoints are stated and slightly developed, the response is really about whether the Bible is important and it does not focus on a Christian's religious life. The personal statement at the end is supported with a simple statement which is not developed.

Response 3

The Bible is important to Christians for several reasons, but this does not mean it is the most important part of their religious life. It is important to Christians because of what it contains, such as the life and teaching of Jesus. It is also important because it is the basis of Christian beliefs and because it is the word of God. As it is the word of God it is a guide to help Christians live a good life. Christians will therefore make it a significant part of their religious life, by reading it regularly, using it as a basis for prayer and meditation, studying it in a Bible class or reading it in church. Other things are important to Christians such as helping the poor, prayer or celebrating the Eucharist. Some Christians would consider the Eucharist to be the more important part of their religious life because they believe Jesus is present in the bread and the wine or that it is transformed into his flesh and blood during the Eucharist. This brings them closer to God than reading the Bible. I think the Bible is the most important part of a Christian's religious life.

Examiner says
This is a satisfactory response and meets the criteria for Level 3. In some respects it is good enough for Level 4 if the justification for the view was developed further. It is reasonably well organised and contains some significant views which are explained well and have evidence to justify them. There is a balance of views. There is good use of technical terms. However the personal response is weak and is not supported with any evidence or argument. This limits the response to Level 3.

ExamCafé

Examiner says

The personal response evaluates the views expressed earlier and comes to a conclusion. The candidate has grasped the significance of the issue. The personal view is backed up by evidence. There is good accurate use of specialist terms and the response is reasonably well organised. This will take the response to level 4.

Understanding exam language

Examiners try to keep questions short, clear and easy to understand. To do this they use words to show what you should do in order to respond to the question. Sometimes a particular word is used to tell you what is required. We call these flag words because they act like flags telling you simply and clearly what is required. Examples of flag words used in Religious Studies exams are:

State:	Usually used in AO1 questions worth 1–3 marks. This means write down a fact about something. E.g. 'State one book of the Bible' – response 'Genesis'.
Give:	This is used instead of 'state' and requires the same sort of response.
List:	This is used instead of 'state' or 'give' and requires the same sort of response.
Describe:	This is used in AO1 questions and means 'tell the examiner factual information about the item or idea'. E.g. 'Describe the interior of a church' means write down factual information about what is to be found inside a church.
Give an account of:	This is asking for the same sort of response as 'describe'.
Explain:	This means show that you understand something. E.g. 'Explain why Christians celebrate Christmas'. This means the examiner wants you to show you understand the reasons Christians give for celebrating Christmas. An 'explain' response will include some knowledge, but the best responses will give reasons and show an awareness of different views on an issue.

Examiner Tip

When answering these questions, ask yourself the question 'why?' as soon as you have written down a reason. There are different levels of explanation and the examiner is looking for depth, not for a superficial level. For example 'they have different calendars' is a reason for different forms of worship, but you need to go on to ask why, and explain why the calendars differ and why this affects worship.

Examiner Tip

'Name' is examiner shorthand for state or give the name of one person. It does not literally mean name someone or something.

Why:	This word is used as shorthand for explain. Put the word explain in front of it and you will know what to do. E.g. 'Why do Christians celebrate Christmas?' is the same as, 'Explain why Christians celebrate Christmas'.
How:	This can be used to ask you for factual information. E.g. 'How do Christians celebrate Christmas?' It can also be used for questions that are asking for understanding where there is a mixture of fact and understanding required. E.g. 'How do Christians react to the problem of world poverty?' The response can be factual about what Christians do or it could be about how Christians will be determined to rid the world of poverty because of their beliefs, which is explanation.
Important:	This word is used frequently in AO1 part d questions and it indicates that you should say why Christians should or should not do/believe something. E.g. 'Explain why the Eucharist is important to Christians' means 'give reasons to explain why some Christians make the Eucharist the main part of their religious life'.

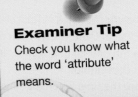

Examiner Tip
Check you know what the word 'attribute' means.

Examiner Tip
Although for the a, b and c parts of a question there is only 1 mark per point, a one word answer is not always possible. You will need to be precise and concise in your response.

Planning and structuring an answer

In some of the Grade Studios you have seen how to build a response. This is really important for the AO1 responses to part d (6 marks) and the AO2 responses to part e (12 marks). In each case follow this structure.

- Check you really know what the question is about. In the AO2 questions work out the key word or words in the statement. E.g. 'Worshipping in church is more important than worship in the home'. The key words are 'more important than'. If the response doe not address this it will not get many marks.
- Make a note of key points to include in AO1 responses and use a spider diagram to note down viewpoints for AO2.
- Begin your response with a brief reference to what the question is asking you to do.
- Write clearly, concisely and in an orderly fashion about the topic or debate. Check all the time that you have explained everything and have referred where appropriate to Christianity.
- Come to a conclusion. In the case of AO1 this may just be – 'so we can see why Christmas is so important'. In the case of AO2 the conclusion should include your personal view and a summing up of the views you have expressed and an evaluation of their significance.
- Write clearly. Manage your time in the exam, so that you can read your responses through to check for sense and accuracy.
- Check spellings and make sure you have used grammar and punctuation. Written communication marks are included in the levels of response.

absolution: the pronouncement by a priest of the forgiveness of sins.

Advent: means arrival or coming. The name given to the 40 days before Christmas.

Anglican Church: churches in full communion with the Archdiocese of Canterbury. Their origins and traditions are linked to the Church of England, and they are part of the Anglican Communion.

annunciation: the time when the Angel Gabriel visited Mary to announce to her that she would give birth to a baby.

anointing of the sick: a ceremony where a priest anoints a sick person with holy oil and says prayers.

Apocrypha: This word means hidden and is used for some of the many books that are not accepted by all Christians as being genuine parts of the scriptures.

apostolic succession: The doctrine (Church teaching) connecting the Church to the original Twelve Apostles.

ascension: the event, 40 days after the resurrection, when Jesus 'ascended into heaven' (see Luke 24 and Acts 1).

Ash Wednesday: the first day of Lent. In some Churches, penitents receive the sign of the cross in ashes on their foreheads.

baptism: a ceremony where water is used as a symbol of washing away sin and starting life as a Christian.

baptistry: a special pool in churches that practise believer's baptism. Or the area of a church in which the font stands.

believer's baptism: baptism of a young person or adult by total immersion in water as a sign that they have committed their life to Christ.

bereaved: feeling a deep a sense of grief and loss at the death of a loved one.

Bethlehem: the birthplace of Jesus.

Bible: From the Greek word 'Biblia' which means books.

Boxing Day: the Feast of St Stephen (popularly called Boxing Day) is celebrated on 26 December.

charity: giving to those in need.

Christ: the anointed one. Messiah is used in Judaism to refer to the expected leader sent by God, who will bring salvation to God's people.

Christening: naming a baby.

Christian: a believer in and follower of Jesus.

Christmas Day: Christmas Day (or Christ's Mass day) is celebrated as the birthday of Jesus.

church: the word has three meanings. (1) The whole community of Christians, (2) the building in which Christians worship and (3) a particular denomination.

clergy: ministers of the church such as priests and vicars.

confession: contrition; (i) One of seven sacraments observed by some Churches whose priest confidentially hears a person's confession; (ii) An admission, by a Christian, of wrong-doing; (iii) A particular official statement (or profession) of faith.

confirmation: a ceremony held when a child is old enough to confirm the promises made on their behalf at baptism.

congregation: religious believers gathered together to take part in worship.

Creed: summary statement of religious beliefs, often recited in worship, especially the Apostles' and Nicene Creeds.

cruciform: this means shaped like a cross.

dedication: a service of welcoming a new baby into a Christian community.

denomination: a group of churches within Christianity which follow a set of beliefs and practices, for example the Church of England.

Easter: central Christian festival which celebrates the resurrection of Jesus Christ from the dead.

ecumenical: a movement that brings different churches together.

epiphany: means 'to reveal'. The name of the Christian festival which celebrates the Magi visiting the infant Jesus.

epistle: From the Greek word for a letter. 21 such letters or epistles, from Christian leaders to Christian Churches or individuals, are included in the New Testament.

eternal life: after death the soul will go to heaven and be eternally in the presence of God.

Eucharist: one of the names for the service associated with the sharing of bread and wine. The word means 'thanksgiving'.

evangelists: the four writers of the Gospels, Matthew, Mark, Luke and John. This word can also be used to describe people who want to spread the message of Christianity to others.

Father: one person of the threefold nature of God.

forgiveness: the teaching of forgiveness forms part of the most important and widely used Christian prayer – the prayer Jesus taught his disciples, commonly known as the Lord's Prayer.

godparents: people chosen by parents to support a child at their baptism and help bring them up to follow a Christian way of life.

Gospels: The books which contain accounts of the teachings and activities of Jesus.

Greek: The original language of the New Testament.

Heaven: the place, or state, in which souls will be united with God after death.

Hebrew: The original language of much of the Old Testament.

Hell: the place, or state, in which souls will be separated from God after death.

Holy Communion/Mass: names associated with the service in which the sharing of bread and wine among the congregation takes place (Eucharist).

Holy Spirit: one person of the threefold nature of God.

hymns: songs that are written to worship or thank God.

immanent: God is close to and involvrd in every part of creation.

incarnate: the doctrine that God took human form in Jesus.

incarnation: the doctrine that God took human form in Jesus Christ.

infant baptism: a ceremony to welcome a baby into the Church; godparents promise to help bring up the child in the Christian faith.

Jerusalem: the place where Jesus died, was buried and rose from the dead.

Jesus of Nazareth: the central figure of Christian history and devotion. The second person of the Trinity.

Last Supper: the Passover meal which Jesus shared with his Disciples on the night before his death.

Lent: penitential season. The 40 days leading up to Easter.

liturgical: service of worship according to a prescribed ritual such as Evensong or Eucharist.

liturgy: the order of a church service.

Lourdes: a place of pilgrimage since 1858 when Bernadette Soubirous experienced a vision while she was walking near a cave in Lourdes.

martyr: someone who is killed because of their beliefs.

Mary: the mother of Jesus, often referred to as The Blessed Virgin or The Virgin. She is classed as a Saint by many Christians.

Nazareth: the place where Jesus grew up.

New Testament: Collection of 27 books forming the second section of the Canon of Christian Scriptures.

Nonconformists: Christian groups which broke away from the Church of England.

Old Testament: That part of the Canon of Christian Scriptures which the Church shares with Judaism, comprising 39 books covering the Hebrew Canon, and in the case of certain denominations, some books of the Apocrypha.

oral tradition: Stories and teachings which have been remembered and passed on by word of mouth for some time before being written down.

orthodox: correct or true beliefs; also refers to denominations.

penance: saying 'sorry' and doing some action to show that you mean it.

Pentecost: annual festival held to remember the coming of the Holy Spirit. It falls seven weeks after Easter.

pilgrimage: journey to a holy place or a religious journey.

Pope: the Bishop of Rome, head of the Roman Catholic Church.

prayer: way of communicating with God to develop a personal relationship with him.

prophecy: This is not foretelling the future so much as explaining what will be the result of human behaviour.

Protestant: That part of the Church which became distinct from the Roman Catholic and Orthodox Churches when their members professed the centrality of the Bible and other beliefs and protested against certain beliefs and practices of the Roman Catholic Church. Members affirm that the Bible, under the guidance of the Holy Spirit, is the ultimate authority for Christian teaching.

purgatory: in some traditions, a condition or state in which good souls receive spiritual cleansing after death, in preparation for Heaven.

reconciliation: the healing of a broken relationship between people and God through Jesus. One of the sacraments in the Roman Catholic and Orthodox churches.

reflection: being quiet and thoughtful, thinking deeply about things.

repent: the first and necessary step towards forgiveness – being truly sorry for the things done or not done and being determined to try to make amends and not to repeat the mistakes (sins).

resurrection: the rising from the dead of Jesus Christ on the third day after the crucifixion.

Roman Catholic: that part of the Church owing loyalty to the Bishop of Rome, as distinct from Orthodox and Protestant Churches. The word 'catholic' means universal or worldwide.

Rome: centre of the Roman Catholic Church.

rosary: this word refers to the set of prayers, including the Hail Mary, or the set of prayer beads themselves.

sacrament: an outward visible sign of an inward spiritual grace, as in e.g. baptism or the Eucharist.

salvation: being saved from the consequences of sin through belief in Jesus.

secular: having a view of the world which is not religious.

sermon: a talk given by the leader of a church service, often to provide an interpretation of the Bible readings or Church beliefs.

seven sacraments: Roman Catholics believe there are seven sacraments which show God at work in people's lives and make people feel close to God. The seven sacraments are baptism, confirmation, marriage, ordination to the priesthood, anointing of the sick, eucharist and reconciliation.

seven sacred mysteries: the Orthodox Church believes there are seven sacred mysteries which show God at work in people's lives and make people feel close to God. The seven sacred mysteries are baptism, chrismation, marriage, ordination, anointing of the sick, the Divine Liturgy and reconciliation.

Shrove Tuesday: celebration by Christians the day before the start of Lent.

Son: one person of the threefold nature of God.

stoup: a small sink or bowl containing holy water.

testament: From a Latin word meaning covenant, which means an agreement.

transcendent: God is beyond the physical/natural world, outside human understanding.

transubstantiation: the belief that during the service of Holy Communion, the bread and wine are changed into the body and blood of Jesus Christ.

Trinity: three persons in one God; doctrine of the threefold nature of God – Father, Son and Holy Spirit.

Virgin Birth: the doctrine of the miraculous conception of Jesus Christ by the Virgin Mary through the power of the Holy Spirit and without the agency of a human father.

Walsingham: a place of pilgrimage in Norfolk, England.

worship: a way of celebrating belief in God, giving thanks and praising him.